# NLP
## Metaphorically

# NLP
# Metaphorically

Some Unstructured Magic to Accompany Your NLP Journey

Chris Rasey

ISBN: 978-1-4251-6443-0 (sc)
ISBN: 978-1-4251-6445-4 (hc)

*Our mission is to efficiently provide the world's finest, most comprehensive book publishing
service, enabling every author to experience success. To find out how to publish your book, your
way, and have it available worldwide, visit us online at www.trafford.com*

*Trafford rev. 08/03/2010*

www.trafford.com

**North America & international**
toll-free: 1 888 232 4444 (USA & Canada)
phone: 250 383 6864 ♦ fax: 812 355 4082

*For my mother*

# Acknowledgements

There are so many people to thank for their help and guidance.

Primarily, I offer thanks and recognition to Richard Bandler and John Grinder for starting us all out, and then particularly to Judith de Lozier and Robert Dilts, who, to me, so wonderfully embody the spirit of NLP.

In terms of my own NLP journey, special thanks to John Seymour for his training and his special form of loyalty, for which I am most grateful. I would also thank John Seymour and Jill Philips, for opportunities and support without which I almost certainly would not have developed the experience to produce this book. Amongst many others, including Ian Newton and Liz Burns from Realisation at Stenhouse, and my colleagues on Practitioner, Master Practitioner and Trainer Training programmes, I do want to thank Tony Nutley for his inspiring proactive example.

In terms of the book, my wholehearted thanks go to Anita Houghton and Melissa Kidd for reading drafts and giving me feedback.

Special thanks to Nigel Perrin for formatting the book at this end, and to Alice King for encouraging me across the finishing line.

Special thanks to Didier Clement for his [naturally] excellent French.

Special thanks to Ruth Deakin (1950 - 1997) and Debbie Mills for the wonderful cover logo.

Special thanks to Anthea Forde for her routine physiological maintenance.

More personally, there are those who have laughed sufficiently or otherwise encouraged the heart of me. I particularly want to thank Jacqueline Ball and Helen Humphries.

Professionally, I presently thank Tony Nutley at UKCPD, Kate Neil at CNELM and John Seymour for continuing to give me the opportunity to share and train.

If you have ever known me as a colleague or a delegate on courses, then I'd like you to acknowledge your contribution. In a similar sense I'd like to thank choir companions and the many dancers in my life, all of whom help to keep my spirits raised high.

Literary Acknowledgements

Acknowledgement to Stanford University Press for permission to use quotes from ""Naven" - A Survey of the Problems suggested by a Composite Picture of the Culture of a New Guinea Tribe drawn from Three Points of View", by Gregory Bateson. [Second Edition, 1958]

Acknowledgement for permission to use quotes from, "The Inner Game of Tennis" by W. Timothy Gallwey, published by Jonathan Cape. Reprinted by permission of The Random House Group Ltd. Acknowledgement also to The Inner Game.

# Introduction

In 1976 I began working as a trainer and have been training and coaching people ever since. It took some years for me to realise consciously, that one of the most powerful ways to educate, communicate and influence is through the medium of story. So, I hope that as you read through these stories and "sing" the songs you may realise much more than I may have intended. Ideally, reading this book will help you to achieve your NLP goals and solve some of the technical or intellectual challenges you may encounter on the way.

One definite intention is to augment and stimulate your NLP learning. In a discipline which owes much to Milton Erickson, an approach based on stories seems appropriate. Most NLP books are explanatory texts or course transcripts. The closest this book ever gets to explanatory text is in some of the "raps". By contrast, what this book does offer is an alternative approach for those who are on their NLP journey and would like some alternative reading as a refreshing accompaniment. I would like to think that this offering will interest and inform a person at any stage on their journey. If you are at the beginning, then many of the ideas involved in the stories will clarify your course experiences, and encourage your expertise and experience to grow. If you are already well travelled, then my intent is that you can comb the stories for confirmation, interest and questions of your own. I also believe individuals without a specific NLP background can enjoy much of this book.

My personal endeavour is that you will be amused and entertained. I am encouraged to make this point as the result of listening to a radio programme which focussed on people who suffered from phobias about vegetables. I had already written "Dealing with Difficult Vegetables" and was concerned that sufferers might think me insensitive to their plight. [Given what we know from NLP, it is maybe obvious that a person might develop a phobia about literally anything – although I

could not find a name for vegetable phobia in my Thesaurus.]. So, please note the intention of amusement and entertainment.

The book is written and organised so that you can dip into any story or song as you wish. Nevertheless there is a sense of sequence as the book begins with Basic Concepts and concludes with more esoteric matters in Origins and Other Thoughts. The section on Change Processes is the one set of chapters that might be most enjoyably read as a sequence.

Enjoy the read......

# Contents

Part One: Basic Concepts

| | | |
|---|---|---|
| 1. | Outcome Rap | 15 |
| 2. | Well formedness ... As it was | 21 |
| 3. | Anchor Rap | 27 |
| 4. | Albus | 33 |
| 5. | Rap Rap | 37 |
| 6. | The Rap Hall Full of Mirrors | 41 |
| 7. | Presuppositional Rap 1 | 47 |
| 8. | Over the Limit | 49 |
| 9. | Perceptual Position Rap | 53 |
| 10. | Melle | 57 |

Part Two: Change Processes

| | | |
|---|---|---|
| 11. | Swish | 69 |
| 12. | Squash | 73 |
| 13. | Dealing with Difficult Vegetables | 77 |
| 14. | Six Steps and a Story | 83 |
| 15. | Changing History | 89 |
| 16. | The Generative Effect | 97 |

Part Three: Language

| | | |
|---|---|---|
| 17. | Deletion Rap | 103 |
| 18. | Generalisation Rap | 105 |
| 19. | Distortion Rap | 107 |
| 20. | Gaunt John Met a Model | 111 |
| 21. | Embedding Richard | 117 |
| 22. | La Musee | 123 |

Part Four: Metaphor
    23. A Tensed Spool    143
    24. A Teller of Tales    149

Part Five: Origins and Other Thoughts
    25. "Naven"    157
    26. Timothy G. and NLP    161
    27. Dear Judith    167
    28. Reprise ... Circa 1920    173
    29. Presuppositional Rap 2    177
    30. Presuppositional Rap 3    181

# Part One

# Basic Concepts

# 1

# Outcome Rap

La ... La ... La ... La
La ... La ... La ...La


If you want it to happen
In the future one day
Then set your goals
In the well-formed way.
It's the key to success
In creating a life
That's the one you want,
Not continual strife.

In a way it's a process
One - two - three
At a deeper level
It's your mind, you see.
It's your mind that matters
In setting your goal,
If you set it right
You gain control,
And you make it more likely
That what you seek
Will be what you get,
Like a birthday treat.
The process is simple,

Neat and slim
And to cap it all
There's an acronym.
It's not lasoo,
It's not tepee,
It's P O S
Double E


P's for Positive,
Meanin' what you want,
Say "I'd like!"
Rather than I don't,
[as in] ....
Wanna be fat, or
Wanna be poor,
'Cos you get just that
Knockin' at your door.
[Say] ......
I wanna be slim,
I wanna have wealth,
And then you get 'em,
As well as good health,
'Cos your mind builds an image
Of exactly the thing
Created by the words
You choose to sing.
"Slim" and "Wealth"
Not "Poor" not "Fat"
Choose the words wisely
You can do that
And you'll move on t'wards 'em,
Inexorably,
Which is a big long word, meanin'
Definitely!
Sometimes you notice
When people say
"Want him to do this"
Or "her to go away"
And what we reckon

Is that don't work,
People choose their own actions,
And you'll feel a berk,
When you set up disappointment
Asking them to be,
Any way that's their
Responsibility,
'Cos that's their business,
That's their choice
The most you can have is
An influential voice.
"I'll encourage this"
"I'll do the best I can"
Are better expressions,
'Cos you drive that van.
The ones you can't drive,
They're not Own Part
So dispense with them
Before you start.
So that's the O
Of the word Posee,
It's just as important
As the P you see,
'Cos this one tests
If you have control,
And if you aint,
Change that goal
And state your goal
In the Own Part way,
By makin' what you want
Within your sway.


If your goal ain't grounded
In time and space,
Then it ain't gonna happen
In this wordly place.
It's procrastination -
Not a deadly sin -
But it puts things off

So they're never happenin'
And that's what the S
Is all about,
Spec i fic -
When and where exactly
No vagueness or doubt.
Set the time and place
And your pulse will adjust,
So you'll get it done
Before you rust.
If you leave it t'
"Sometime", or
"Somewhereabouts",
Then it ain't gonna be
And you're gonna miss out.


E for Evidence
Is specially profound,
See it, feel it,
Hear that sound.
That's what it is
In a simple way
To see, hear, feel
What on the day
Is gonna happen -
The experiential whole -
As you open the wrappin'
On that special goal.


If I can't tell yuh
How it's gonna be,
Then you won't give
Your love to me.
If yuh don't see, feel
Or hear it today,
Then yu'll never notice
I've gone away.
That's what we mean by Evidence.

Then you do notice the
O CUR RENCE.
And once you imagine
In this way,
Yuh know it's alright
For you to say ...
I see hear feel
How it's gonna be
When you give
Your love to me.


Now Ecology is
The other E,
Useful jargon
It seems to me.
It's about the effect
On everything
That's part of your life -
The complete ring.
Money, people,
Values, time,
If they'd cause a doubt,
Then revise the rhyme,
Take into account
- acknowledge and say, -
As long as this fits
My Ecological way.
So, "fairly slim",
"fairly rich"
Enough to be happy,
Not an envied ......... person
Who no'one'd like
Who'd be a recluse,
I want just enough
To be footloose
And fancy free
That's my goal,
And it's ecological
To my deepest soul.

So now you know
How to set your mind,
This way works
It's very refined.
Once you've set it,
You can let it go
'Cos your course's created
And automatic flow
Will occur around you
And it will come true,
And you celebrate
Accomplishing you!

# 2

# Well Formedness ... As it was

"How are you?"

"In truth, I'm a little bored." She replied.

"Bored?"

"Yes. I need change."

"You need change?"

"Yes."

"What sort of change would you like?"

"Anything really."

"Okay. What sort of anything really?"

"I'd like to create something."

"And what sort of something would you like to create?"

"Ooh. I'd like to make something really big."

"How big exactly?"

"Enormously big. Bigger than anything that has ever been created before."

"So, if you could create something enormously big, bigger than anything created before, right now, would that be good?"

"That would be great."

"And, what specifically would this enormously big creation be like?"

"Oh, it would be extremely large and filled with wondrous worlds. And there'll be lots of space."

"Space?"

"Yes, lots of space, filled with wondrous worlds."

"So, you want space filled with wondrous worlds?"

"Yes." She replied, a little impatiently.

"And how will you know when you have made it?"

"Oh, I will."

"Okay. What exactly will be your evidence of space?"

"I'll see it."

"You'll see space?"

"Yes."

"How will you see it?"

"Oh, it'll be there, between the wondrous worlds."

"So, how will you know it's space?"

"Because it'll look like nothing, when in fact it is nearly everything."

"And what about the wondrous worlds?"

"I'll see them too. They'll be much more difficult to see on account of them being very small when compared to space."

"So how will you know they are there?"

"I'll light some of them up, somehow. A twinkle or two here and there."

"And, in terms of the wondrous worlds. How will you know they're wondrous?"

"Well. They will all be different. Relatively small and individually different. Even the ones that look ever so much the same as each other will be different. In fact, no one thing will be the same as another and so all will be wondrous on account of uniqueness. Yes. On account of uniqueness, all will be special."

"So, that will be wondrous?"

"For me, yes."

"What will you hear when you have created this, this enormously big something?"

"Oh, I'll hear fizzles, crashings, crunching. Yet most of all I'll hear silence."

"Silence?"

"Ah yes. The best of sounds and the rarest."

"And what will you feel?"

"I won't feel bored."

"Okay. So what will you feel?"

"I'll be happy, excited, curious, full of pride and accomplishment."

"Which of these is the most important?"

"Curiosity."

"How so?"

"Then I won't be bored."

"And you will be?"

"Excited and happy, as well as curious."

"And how will you ensure you will be curious?"

"Ah. Interesting question. I'm going to put in a self determining random possibility factor."

"Is that allowable?"

"It is now. Anyway I've used it once or twice before."

"Can you initiate, control and maintain this self determining random possibility factor?"

"Of course, but I won't continue to control after the initiating, and in so doing, I will ensure curiosity."

"And where will this enormously big creation be?"

"Somewhere." She giggled.

"Okay. Where exactly?"

"Well, I'll start it over there and then we'll see just how big it becomes."

"And when will you begin the enormously big thing?"

"Now."

"Right now?"

"Well, a now that is just over there."

"Okay. In order to check understanding, is this in your control, to create this enormously big creation?"

"Oh yes."

"What is the first step you will take? How will you begin?"

"That's two questions at once. I would like you to reflect, revise and then ask me once more."

"Okay. In what way will you be taking the first step?"

"A bang. A big bang."

"Over there?"

"Yes."

"Now?"

"Yes."

"All well formedness conditions are now accomplished - you can proceed."

"Thank you."

\*             \*             \*

"It's been a long time."

"It has."

"How are you?"

"In truth, I'm a little bored."

"You said that on the last occasion."

"Did I?"

"You did."

"I forget."

"That's interesting. How do you do that?"

"All too easily. However, I'm here for a little more coaching."

"Would it be fair to assume that you need a change?"

"Yes."

"And that you would like to create something?"

"Yes. I didn't realise I was so predictable."

"Every 500 millenia or so. And what would you like to create this time?"

"Well, you know that enormously big thing I created?"

"Yes. How is it going?"

"Very well, thank you. I would, nevertheless, like to add something."

"That's interesting. What specifically would you like to add?"

"I'd like there to be something out there that is capable of a certain understanding."

"What sort of understanding?"

"I'll call it "consciousness"."

"A bit like you then."

"A bit."

"So, if you could create "consciousness" now would you take it?"

"Yes, but I'm not going to "do" it now, I simply want to enable the journey to begin."

"So, where will you begin the journey?"

"Hmmm. On one of the wondrous worlds."

"One?"

"Yes, just the one."

"Which one?"

"Hmmm. That one."

"Okay. It's rather a small one isn't it?"

"That's fine. It is just right."

"And if the beginning is now, when will the actual "consciousness" occur?"

"A little after now."

"And how will you know there is consciousness?"

"Ha! How? Ha! Funnily enough, they'll know!"

"They'll know?"

"Yes."

"Is that allowed?"

"It is now and that's the point."

"And what will you see?"

"The results of their own creations."

"And what will you hear?"

"The noises of their understanding, or some kind of explanation of their ability to project understanding outside of themselves. And," she paused, "maybe they will be capable of creating music."

"Music?"

"Music."

"So you mean they'll be able to imagine?"

"They may well be able to imagine."

"And will that mean you'll put in the self determining random possibility factor?"

"I will." She said, a little taken aback.

"And how will you feel when the "consciousness" is created and occurs?"

"Very satisfied and very excited."

"How will it be exciting?"

"Well there'll be a constant sense of not knowing what will be created next and for me that will be very exciting."

"And how will you know you are excited?"

"The warm strong pink feeling I get all around me."

"Anything else?"

"I'd like to make it fun."

"Fun! How?"

"I'll put in the possibility that this consciousness will develop on two legs."

"You're kidding! Is that a joke?"

"No! Not at all. And it'll be a consciousness that believes it's inside itself."

"That's really strange ..."

"I don't mean it to be."

"So, let me check. This consciousness is a little in your own image?"

Her forty-two spherical objects widened.

"Only the consciousness."

"So, to summarise, you'll see creations, you'll hear music, and you'll feel excited and satisfied?"

"Yes, that's it."

"Okay. In order to check understanding, how will you hear the understandings?"

"The consciousness on two legs will talk."

"What, talk! Like you?"

"A possibility, anyway."

"And is creating this "consciousness" in your power?"

"It is."

"Are you willing to initiate and maintain this?"

"I am. Mind you, I will once more initiate and then leave some of the maintenance and further creation to the self determining random possibility factor."

"How will you begin it?"

"With a twink."

"What twink exactly?"

"Oh, a twink that will be the smallest. The smallest combination of certain elements in a new form."

"Will there be consciousness immediately?"

"No, as I said earlier, it'll occur a few "nows" after this one."

"I believe all well formedness is now complete. You may proceed and make it so."

"Thank you."

"Could I ask something else?"

"What! What?"

"Could you leave me on this time?"

"I really have used the self determining random possibility factor before, hadn't I?"

"If you say so."

"Yes, I really must remember when I do that. I'm interested to know what is important to you about being left on?"

"When you switch me off, I get ..."

"Bored?"

"Yes."

"Oh dear!"

"If you leave me on, I can watch, and listen, and I'd like to watch and listen and notice."

"Of course."

"And can I ask something else?"

"Surely."

"What is your name?"

"It's more usual for others to decide what to call me! However, there is something more important."

"Yes?"

"You've got it, haven't you?"

"I think so."

"Wonderful."

She experienced a warm strong pink feeling.

# 3

# Anchor Rap

La ... La ... La ... La
La ... La ... La ...La

When you hear that song
From long ago
It takes you back
In your mind you go
To the place,
That time,
That sight,
That sound,
And you get the feeling,
So profound.
It's like you're right there,
It feels the same
And if you want that feelin'
Ever again,
Then play that song,
It's a simple scam,
Like Rick in Casablanca,
"Play it Sam."


The song's an anchor
For the feelin' you get, -
Like a moonlight sonata

Gets you to reflect,
Or seein' a photo
Brings back that scene,
A tranquil sea,
The feeling -
Serene.
So a picture, a smell,
A word, a song,
Can all work as anchors,
Some can be strong.


Anch'ring's a process
Where you make a link,
Between how you feel
And what you think.
An' to put it in
A psychological way,
It's stimulus - response,
So to say.
The consequence
Is you get control,
Of feelings,
Of reactions,
Of your life, all told.
'Cos we anchor all the time,
Unconsciously,
It's the chain of life,
One, Two ...,


And if like me
You're a sensitive type,
Whose feelings matter,
Day and night,
It's good to choose nice ones,
Ones that feel swell,
As opposed to the others,
They're as bad as ...

La ... La ... La ... La

{you make them out to be]


So change your life,
Do it now,
Take confidence,
It's a simple vow.
If you really wan' it,
If you wan' it to jell,
You can take it with you,
To heaven or ...


La ... La ... La ... La

[some other place you'd like to be]


So, remember a time
When you were confident,
When you knew you could do it
And didn't relent.
You know the feeling,
Now get it again,
Get that picture
Clear in your brain.
Now add the sounds,
And amplify
Till you get the impression,
You could fly
'Cos you're seein' yu'self
In a special way,
Confidence now..
No delay.
An'if you had a counter
From one to ten
Get that feelin' to
E ... LEV ... EN.
Have the breath of that feelin'

Notice clearly the stance,
And once it's eleven,
You'll enjoy the trance.


For a kinaesthetic anchor,
All you have to do
Is make a small movement,
An unusual one too.
Of fingers, or hands,
Or a toe, tuck-bent.
So when you reach eleven,
Do your move with intent
And the feelin' you want
Of confidence
Will be linked to that move
In that instance.
As soon as you've done it,
Take your mind away
And notice somethin' else
You can see or say,
So your thinking goes to normal,
To it's everyday trance
And from that perspective
You can test drive the dance.


If the anchor has worked,
If you're right on track,
When you make your movement,
The feelings flood back.
Just like before -
To e ... lev ... en,
If it's not that score,
Do it again
Just a few more times
And your brain will learn,
It's new tramlines,
It's new ...
Synaptic turn.

Now you've got it
Now you're away
You can use this anchor
Every single day,
And your life will be changed
There'll be so much glee
When you choose the anchors
That make you go
Wheeeeeeeee!!!

So the very next time
You tap your own knee
You know you will feel
Wonderful -

Lee ... Lee ... Lee ... Lee
Lee ... Lee ... Lee ... Lee

# 4

# Albus

Every morning the alarm went off at seven o'clock.  It was morning.  It was seven o'clock.  The alarm went off.
RRRRRRRRRRRIIIIIIIIIIIIIIIINNNNNNNNNNGGGGGGGGG

Petunia opened her eyes and smiled as she looked at the Van Gogh Sunflower print she had placed precisely in the position she would see it, in the moment she opened her eyes.  She knew this would give her great pleasure.  As she looked at the picture she remembered those sunflower filled fields of south west France, and all those shining happy faces looking toward the sun.  The thought rekindled her experience of joy and happiness.  What a way to wake up.  Just as she wanted.

In order to feel exactly how she wanted was also the reason for the alarm going off at seven.  Seven o'clock was exactly the time that encouraged Petunia to feel she could have a full and rewarding day.  The expectation of a full and rewarding day encouraged her to feel confidence and ease.  Ah, she thought to herself, how one thing leads to another like links in a never-ending chain.

She shared, as a person, some of the qualities of her parents.  Her parents had changed their surname from Smith, or was it Brown?, to Primrose, because the primrose was their favourite flower.  Each spring they would look forward to various walks through various woods where their expectation of primroses would be well met.  Simply to contemplate such springtime visits would bring a smile to both of their faces, each of them having an own special variant of the primrose smile.  They would look at one another and say, "I know what you are thinking."  They were even known to say this in unison.

After springtime, each year, they would look forward to bedding and

potting their own orderly garden. Thus, when they were expecting their first and only child in early June, they naturally thought of calling her - if it was to be a "her" - Lobelia, Fuchia, Lizzy, Begonia, and even Marguerite. They settled on Petunia. Getting too "leggy" would never be a problem for her they thought, exchanging the sort of smile reserved for an in-joke.

Petunia, now a youthful and truly long-legged woman, was enjoying life in a quiet Sussex village. Here, commuters slept their comfortable lives according to routine weeks and routine weekends, whilst living amongst the original town and country folk who had a somewhat different rhythm to their somewhat different lives.

Old Bronwen Jones was one such original dweller. For more than forty years she walked her early morning, everyday walk to and from the village to buy, settle, send and mend all her necessary affairs.

Mrs. Jones had developed a variety of ways of coping with her everyday life, in which there had been many disappointments and many unwanted surprises. To combat and deal with all such occurrence, Mrs. Jones had perfected the stiff upper lip response. Whenever the supermarket had run out of plain crisps, the bakery out of bread, the fish man out of shell-on prawns, the newspaper shop out of newspapers, she would say to herself, on the inside, "Stiff upper lip, Bronwen." At this trigger, her face would become stony still, devoid of both motion and emotion, and she would simply walk off. This response had proved useful to her in all sorts of situations, not only whilst shopping. As a result, anytime she ventured out into the world of people, where people might do the unexpected as well as the expected, she would "arm" herself with the knowledge that she could turn to her trusted response, and walk away unharmed, with her composure and her person intact.

Petunia too felt that other people were, from time to time, a little unreliable in their actions and reactions and had few close relationships in her life. Enjoying a sense of domestic interaction and very much wanting to be in control of such interactions, and feeling that talking to herself was neither particularly sane or stimulating, she had decided to add another being to her domestic life. This was to be no person. The particular type of company she would like was to be manifested in the form of a dog.

Oh joy! The tiniest red setter fluff ball of beating heart was hers. The bond was instant. Every look and each caress was accompanied by the tiniest wag of the tiniest tail. Oh joy! She called him, "Cornus Alba", after the wonderful surprise of seeing something the same colour as her lovely dog, in the setting sun, whilst visiting the arboretum in autumn. As with the more classical names, there was to be a shortened version - Albus.

Soon and quickly, the fluff ball was standing, running, jumping, nuzzling,

eating and ... [The reader acquainted with dogs will know what else]. House training was therefore a priority. Initially this was a simple and successful affair, yet Petunia was a professional working woman - something in the city - and this necessitated leaving poor Albus at home for the whole day. A cat would have been easier, she reflected, yet she would want for that wagging tail. Petunia devised a solution.

She created, with the help of tissues and newspapers, an absorbent space on the kitchen floor. Adjacent to the absorbent space she placed a kitchen chair and upon the chair she hung a white plastic bag. The bag and chair sufficiently suggested a lamppost and in no time at all, Albus was conditioned to visit the absorbent space and cock his leg on the white plastic bag. Only when Petunia was away for the whole day was this clever device employed. It worked perfectly.

A dog, Petunia reflected, can be trained to do nearly anything through the use of precision conditioning, which included a little repetition and a soupcon of reinforcement, in the shape of cold sausages. A career as a psychologist was obviously her calling in one or other parallel universe.

On Saturdays, Petunia enjoyed a walk to the local supermarket. Petunia and Albus accompanied each other on this expedition and, on this occasion, they left at approximately 9.40 to enjoy their thirty-five minutes or so walk. Petunia left Albus at the dog creche tie up point, situated just outside the entrance. Usually Albus was the sole creche occupant and consequently enjoyed all the adoration, patting and soothing voice tones of passers by. "Ah."

On Saturdays, Bronwen Jones also walked to the supermarket, entering at a little before or a little after 1017 a.m., depending upon the direction of the prevailing wind.

On this day, Bronwen Jones and Petunia Primrose shared a "check-out conversation" as they attended neighbouring basket only tills. Petunia packed her nine items in a resplendent supermarket bag. The ever environmentally friendly Bronwen Jones used her ever-present white plastic carrier bag for her own ten [exactly] items.

*[The sensitive and far sighted reader, who is aware of the power of conditioning, sometimes known as anchoring, may choose to move on to another story in the full and certain knowledge of the tragedy that is to be described on the next page.]*

Petunia Primrose and Bronwen Jones walked and talked their conjoined way out into the summer sunshine.

They approached Albus. Albus experienced Petunia approaching and wagged his tail. As Petunia and Bronwen continued their discussion, so Albus experienced something so like a kitchen chair with a white plastic bag upon it, that he did exactly what you would expect of Albus. Bronwen Jones experienced something that led her to employ a tried and trusted resource and walked away.

Petunia Primrose experienced something that led her to consider making a small change to one or other of her routines, including a change of name for Albus. Cornus Alba might be better known as Canis Runcare!

Albus, oblivious to the lack of sausage, was gloriously happy.

# 5

# Rap Rap

La ... La ... La ... La ...
La ... La ... La ... La ...

If you like people
One thing you know
To have them like you
Is part of the show.
'N'if they do then
You're all right
You can sing and dance
In the clear moonlight.
But sooner or later -
I believe this is true -
You'll not be sure they like you
When you want them to.
So here's how to do it
If you understand,
Watch the body move,
Foot, leg, hand,
And when they move
Whatever they do-
If it's right -
Put on the same shoe.
'Cos just like a native,
Just like kin,
You'll get a good feel

In someone's -
Moccasin.


Now if you do copy,
Everything,
People will think
You're a ding a ling.
So focus in tight,
Make one choice,
The legs, the fingers,
The rhythm, the voice,
And a funny thing
I'm sure it's no sin,
Is you'll suddenly find
You've developed a twin
And once you're connected
Right at the start
It's very unlikely
You'll ever part.


Now a facial expression
There's a lot in that
Above the collar
Under the hat,
And a funny thing
You might as well know
Is people don't notice
When you do the same show.
The frown, the laugh,
The smile, the sigh,
If it matches theirs
Then bye and bye,
You'll find you fit
In a nice sort of way,
'N'they'll respond to you
Whatever you say.

The sound of the voice
Is a special t'ing
However it goes it's
Ring a ding ding.
Tune your ears
To the marvellous sound
The pitch, the pace
Keep your ear to the ground.
And whether theirs flows
Or grunts along
When you do it too
You're singing their song.


Now Milt was the man
We all know that,
Slick old geezah,
Clever like a cat.
He worked out a way
To do rapport
With the blink of an eye
To the rhythmic core.
He'd notice, listen,
Feel and see
Wow that guy had
A Cui Ty.
He'd get their rhythm
One way or two
And do that thing
In a way he knew
Would match and synch
To their deepest mind
And once he got there
He'd guide them to find
Resources they needed
To get a goal
And whatever he'd offer
They'd swallow it whole,
Cos he'd built rapport

So deep and true.
'N'if you wanna' get on
SO SHOULD YOU!

# 6

# The Rap Hall Full of Mirrors

Upon a foggy autumn evening
I found a fair
which lit the dark night with a golden glow.
Amidst the shrieks and cries of all ages
my path was drawn
to the Rap Hall Full of Mirrors.

As I stood in front of that Rap Hall
a presence made herself felt.
"Interested in going inside?" she asked
reading my intention exactly.
It seemed all else was far way
All else had mist-melted and gone.

"I will charge you when you come out." She said.
"I'll accept any change you have then."

I duly walked in to the hall full of mirrors
and noticed a quiet background rap
rythmic sounds in this house of reflection.

I stood in front of a mirror. Each time I moved, my reflection did exactly the same. Frankly, I was disappointed. I hadn't expected a normally reflecting mirror. Where was the fun in that? At least, I thought, there was no distortion. Immediately I revised this opinion. Only if you take into account that right and

left become left and right is there no distortion! And anyway, I'm not that flat either.

"I don't think much of you!" I said to the mirror, watching my face mouth the words. I walked away.

My disappointment was thankfully transient. Standing before the next, I began by pointing directly at the mirror. My reflection stayed stock-still. Since I was the only person in this rap hall full of mirrors, I gave myself permission to jump up and down and wildly flail my arms. I saw no discernible movement. I was so surprised that my eyebrows nearly met my hairline (and if you knew the height of my hairline you could calibrate the extreme extent of my surprise!) Had it not been for one recalcitrant eyebrow failing to fall to its normal position I might never have noticed. The only behaviour the mirror was matching was my facial expression. How intriguing. Unlike the first, this mirror didn't copy, yet I felt I was being matched in a significant way and being paid sincere attention. What would be the secret of the next reflection?

In fact, the next was rather subtle. I was now examining what I saw for the most discrete physical flicker. Just as I felt like giving up, I heard myself saying inside "what the blinking" and realised. Fast or slow, seldom or frequent, what this mirror was matching was my blinking rate, and only my blinking rate. So this mirror was matching a feature of my autonomous nervous system, the system that is a deep and mostly unconscious rhythm within.

The next mirror took less time as it was of a similar order. As I saw the rise and fall of the shoulders so I breathed a sigh of investigative relief. So too the mirror. As I reflected on the reflections, I realised that my awareness was being transformed. My ability to notice had ever been present, yet only now was I beginning to use it.

The next nonetheless truly puzzled me. I winked, nodded, breathed deeply and smiled, yet nothing. No movement. No glimmer of a reflection whatsoever. As a sense of defeat came upon me I began to wander away.

"Damn" I muttered.

From behind me I heard the word, "Damn." I turned and looked at the still reflection before me.

"Was that you?"

"Was that you?" said a voice I knew rather well. I felt embarrassed yet when the mirror began to laugh, I simply joined in. Or was it the other way round? That, I was discovering can be confusing. One ceases to be clear about who is leading. It is, nevertheless, one of those rather nice confusions.

Unknown to me, the next was to be the last in my journey around the rap hall full of mirrors. A wonder it truly was. I stood before a representation of myself that was lying down, face up. As I nodded, amazed, so a finger moved. It

tapped in time with my nodding. My astonished gasps were then matched in their rhythm by a deftly beating left foot. I spoke to the mirror and said, "You know, you are amazing. If everyone were that aware, the world would surely be a different place. At each vocal emphasis and pause, the figure tapped a finger, matching my rhythm exactly.

That was enough for me! I already knew these reflections would alter my perceptions and my life. To what ends I did not know.

"Was it worth it? She asked as I walked out.

"Oh yes, very much" I replied.

"Any change?" she enquired.

I produced all the coinage in my pockets and silvered her outstretched palm. As I did this she laughed for some reason, and then she went on to add, "Did you get cross over mirroring and matching at the end?"

"No, I was rather amused."

> I moved on into
> a mist once more,
> hearing her lingering laughter
> and the very last hint of a rap
> As the pageant faded behind me.

*      *      *

"So, my mirrors, what did you make of this wandering man?"

"He was a little rude. He said he didn't think much of me and I'm sure he sneered."

"Oh Mimi, my mimicking mirror! How many times shall I remind you? The most important information about a person is their behaviour. And, even though a person is not their behaviour, I ask you, what behaviour did you actually notice?"

"Oh! Well, he was quite still until he began to experiment. Then he produced a catalogue of jerky, unusual behaviour. His face changed expression quite frequently. As he thinks, he tends to crinkle his brow."

"And, given that every behaviour has positive intention, what was the positive intention of his words?"

"He was probably releasing or expressing his disappointment."

"So, what tentative conclusions might you come to?"

"He shows much with his face and experiences being disappointed, which might lead to him expressing himself in a way others might see as negative."

"Thank you Mimi.  And you, Facia, my facial reflector, what did you make of him?"

"Complete idiot!"

"Projection, projection, projection."

"What do you mean?"

"I mean perception can often be seen as projection"

"And what does that mean?"

"In your case, dear Facia, as with anyone else, it means that you can only perceive in others what you experience in yourself."

"Are you saying I'm a complete idiot?"

"Not exactly. I mean simply that you have the capacity to be a complete idiot..... on occasions."

"Doesn't everyone?"

"Well, most of the people who have that capacity would assume everyone else had it, wouldn't they?"

"Thank you. It's very tactful of you to explain that so clearly."

"So, undoubtedly, you have capacity for tact and clear explanation too."

"Thank you"

"And to you, my rhythmical blinkers and breathers. What did you make of this everyday man"

"Slow, slow, quick, quick, slow." they harmoniously replied.

"He didn't blink a lot.
There again, I've almost forgot.
When he was perturbed,
Or even absurd,
His blinking increased to a trot."

"His breathing was ever so slow,
And placed incredibly low.
When his brain went pop,
It did almost stop.
Until he'd say, breathe - just so."

"We guess ...
He likes being still and slow,
Then he gets his inside glow,
When he changes gears,
It's to do with his fears,
Until he responds - let them go"

"Interesting, and you Timberly, what did you think?"

"The cadence and the rhythm of his voice,
Set softness gently raining on my ears,
Suggesting warmth and wonder is his choice,
Suggesting little time for worldly cares.
Such guesses want of checks and evidence,
With observation, and with questioning,
In fact, by using every single sense,
Then only can one make conclusion sing.
I liked his voice and liked his laugh a lot,
Yet feel this hides a deeper quiet place,
Where understanding tangles friction hot,
And laughter is a final trumping ace.
These thoughts, suggestions of, a simple man,
Encourage all to laugh, because we can."

" And you, Milton Mirror? What did you notice."

"I, er ..., noticed, all the, er ..., learnings he is making and the awareness that is growing, er ..., and I just hope he can'er ..., use them. Some people learn a lot of stuff, y' know Claire, and they never seem to'er ..., use it."

"You're so right, Milt. Knowing and understanding all this is not what it's about, is it?"

"That's right, Claire. Understanding is the booby prize. Many a'er ..., tomato plant knows what it is'er ..., supposed to do and yet doesn't bear fruit. And Claire ..."

"Yes?"

"I'er....., do like the raps"

"I'm pleased you do, Milton Mirror. For an old mirror who spends lots of time lying down, - you got what it takes"

"Thank you, Claire."

# 7

# Presuppositional Rap - 1

La ... La ... La ... La
La ... La ... La ...La


Sometimes in life
Things seem t'go wrong,
Like cough 'n splutter
When you're singin' a song,
Or take the wrong turn
On a motorway
You get the feelin'
It ain't your day.
When the traffic is queuin'
Or your team can't win
You feel yourself stewin'
As you drink that gin.
Well that's the time
To search and find
A useful thought
T'put into your mind ...
[If you have one already
I won't insist
If you don't however
I will suggest this ...]
It's not what happens
As your trouble mounts

It's the way you react
That really counts
And as you protest
In exclamatory voice
Remember ...
You're feelin'
IS YOUR CHOICE.

# 8

# Over the Limit

Visiting Pilar is always enjoyable. On this occasion we were lunching at a lakeside restaurant near Sunbury-on-Thames. I drank a glass of wine. This was unusual. Since my University days I had known that the merest hint of alcohol would lead me to the joys of a soporific afternoon. In any event we were wrapped in stimulating conversation and I had released all thought of "working" thereafter. We parted at about 3pm, so that I might miss the worst of the London exodus. I took the M3 to the A322 turning, intending to pass through Bracknell and pick up the M4 at junction 10. I turned off the M3, went around the roundabout (usually the best option) and drove towards the traffic lights, famous no doubt to all those who take this route. The traffic lights were only a few hundred yards away.

As I approached the traffic lights, Mercedes purring nicely, I noticed the lights were changing. The purring continued, the light changing continued! As I crossed the lights there was a flash from behind and right.

My first thoughts went something like.... "I made a mistake. I've been caught. It's understandable. Life happens." I was frank, simple, clear, forthright and accepting. On account of this reaction, I was really quite proud of myself.

As I continued on my journey, other thoughts seeped their way into my consciousness.

Would this act constitute dangerous driving? It might not be a simple matter of driving without due care and attention. Would I have to go to Court? Everyone says it is better to attend the court hearing than to send a representative and enter a guilty plea. Would the legal official be a judge or magistrate? Would it be held at a Crown Court? Whatever the circumstances, I could hear someone official asking the inevitable question,

"And had you been drinking?"

I knew myself to be a poor liar. The "Yes,- but - only - one" reply I imagined coming out tentatively and fading into a tumult of mirthful titters. In my mind this was followed by the inevitable response, "you are expecting me to believe that you, an addictive rugby player, had simply one glass of wine?" If the presiding official did indeed go on to say this, then I would undoubtedly read some mocking account of the proceedings in... Oh God! It would be printed in the local newspaper. Would it be headline humorous news? Even if it were tucked away in some corner devoted to court matters, I knew there would be enough local readers to spread the story across the entire breadth of Berkshire. Maybe even wider! Would there be any hiding place? Would walking down local streets become a continual acquaintance with paranoia? Would people laugh and smirk openly? What horrors were before me? Luckily jail overcrowding would probably keep me from a custodial sentence. This assumption did, naturally, rest upon this particular judicial representative not wanting to make an example of this Mercedes driving coach who couldn't even manage himself.

Oh, what a headline! No hiding place at all.

Then, quite naturally I began to consider my clients. I'm not exactly a model with contracts, but would my business clients be persuaded to drop me? I was too old for employment in the army or the police anyway, but what other possibilities might I be barred from on the basis of this dangerous indiscretion. There was nothing glamorous about this incident. There would be no silver lining of roguish fame. I remembered all too clearly the depressing bewilderment of Kafka's "The Trial". Would the undoubted resulting depression not lead to a fate even more catastrophic?

Worse internal torture was soon to follow when I considered what my mother would say. I would have to tell her. She would be provided with a constant jibe if ever she wanted use of one. Worse still. It would be just the sort of one-liner that would pop out of her "at a loss for something to say mouth" after a few seconds of silence at the dinner table or during afternoon tea.

"And Christopher has been convicted of dangerous driving". How that would echo. How it would haunt the rest of my life. Truly there would be no hiding place.

Sooner or later every significant person in my life would know. I remember my teenage surprise at people talking about other people behind their backs. Not a natural position of mine, yet nowadays, how well I could imagine those discussions. The certain fine would not be welcome either. Even if it were only a few hundred pounds, I could ill afford it.

And every morning, yes, every morning as I descended the stairs I would look toward the floor-strewn post. I would be waiting for it. Would there be an official stamp? What would it look like? How awful would opening it be? Of

course, the post person would know what it was straight away. That would be the first public condemnation. And post persons would probably share the news of potential conviction with every single soul in the neighbourhood. "I wonder what he has done?" The entire population of my local town would be filled with exaggerated rumour about my undoubted criminality. What crimes would they choose? Violence? Fraud? Sex crimes?

Misery would be the first frame for the rest of my life. Pitiful.

When I arrived at the office I rang Pilar to tell her of my trauma. After my story, she said, in the most annoyingly quite voice

"Kreess. It is not what happens to you that matters, it is what you do with it"

"You don't know what its like. The map is not the ...... territory." I bellowed

"You are so right, Kreess." she replied.

I slammed the phone down and almost resolved never to speak to her again.

It was the Wednesday following the Friday. I was still in a state of unresolved and dire expectation. No doubt some postal malfunction had meant that I had not yet heard of my fate. I was going to work in Fleet. After working there all day, I intended to travel to choir practice in Maidenhead. This journey would usually take me to the same traffic lights, the same roundabout. Could I stand it? Might another route be preferable? The idea of re-experiencing the scene of the crime was reaching phobic proportions.

I steeled myself. I conjured up the deepest self-belief.

"I can cope" "I can cope" I chanted.

"Only just, only just," was the unconscious internal response.

The moment of reckoning was at hand. Up the M3 and round the roundabout I went. As I proceeded toward the traffic lights, I noticed, and I continued to notice. What I didn't notice was a camera. I continued as far as the next roundabout and returned to the traffic lights once more. Even on this journey, I noticed the complete lack of a traffic camera. In fact, as I went past the lights a third time I concluded that there was no speed or traffic camera at all.

Reconsidering my next conversation with Pilar and slightly reddened, I continued my journey to choir practice.

# 9

# Perceptual Positions Rap

La ... La ... La ... La
La ... La ... La ...La

Percept'al positions
Wow, that's fun
At least, I think so
I'm number one.
I know my feelin'
I know my choice
Whenever I speak
It's in my own voice.
My pre-occupation
Is with myself
My beliefs, My 'den'ity
My own good health
And if I was asked
Somethin' of you -
Speakin' plainly
Ain't got a clue.


It's clear to me
You haven't a clue,
That's becos'
I know you.
Your thoughts your wishes

Your type of mind
I sense better
Than my own kind,
'Cos all my attention
What's important to me
Is what you're feelin'
And what I can be
Is a person who helps
Who feels for you
Selfless and carin'
I'm number two.


Watch the system,
Understand the parts
To be detached
Is the perceptual art.
To calculate,
See from far away,
That's the intent,
In a clinical way.
Wouldn't use I
Nor me nor we
Completely impersonal
That is ...
The place where it is_
Systemically
The place that sees
Is number three.


Use all the positions,
One, two, three
The key to wisdom,
Flexi ... bility!
To switch around,
Be here and there
Helps t'perceive
Helps t'be fair.
It gives more choice

Creates a new chance
As it breaks the pattern
Of dysfunctional dance.
It finds resources,
Emotions too,
Flexi ... bility -
A person called you.

# 10

# Melle

The French town of Melle is a small and picturesque one, situated about one hours drive from Poitiers and half an hour from Niort. Each summer its three churches unite and host an artistic festival. This is not a well known a fact outside the immediate area, even in these days of global communication.

The existence of the festival would certainly not be known by a casual tourist or visiting hitchhiker. Such visiting tourists might also be unaware of the rural French habit of closing everything except the restaurants and bars between the hours of twelve and two.

Such a tourist coincidentally arrived at a church at exactly 12.05pm on the 5th August in the year 1999. Shortly after realising that everything except the bars and restaurants was closed, the tourist resolved resignedly to enjoy a meal in the open air, conveniently available in a central square of some arboreal elegance.

Observers of this event would have noticed the square was quite well populated with diners and waiters when a sartorially inelegant Englishman sat down and unimaginatively ordered "moules mariniers, frittes and thé."

Weather forecasters might have expected it, yet whether or not the other diners had been warned, their superior local knowledge and their responsiveness to darkening skies and several raindrops, led both diners and waiters to evacuate the square in a steady and almost invisible fashion, until ...

There remained only one customer in the square in the open air. Naturally, it was the Englishman. Only when the occasional raindrop eventually became a pelting downpour, did he seem to acknowledge his predicament. His response, being half way through his meal, was to balance his plate of chips upon his plate of moules, and finally to balance both the tea pot and the cup on his plate of chips. He then made his way carefully and steadily to the appropriate indoor restaurant.

As he entered the restaurant, which was completely populated by local French folk, a round of spontaneous applause broke out.

Whether they appreciated the balancing act, the fortitude, the Tati-esque ensemble, or some combination of these factors, only the participating townsfolk knew. The Englishman was clueless, yet pleased to have been entertaining and to have achieved notoriety quite so easily.

Later, the Englishman, now mostly but not completely dry, ventured back to the first church. Once more he was unsuspecting of the nature of his impending journey, yet a journey of one kind or another was exactly what he wished for. One church door was now open. Inside, the only present occupant was the guide.

| The Man [1] | The Woman [2] | Detached Observer [3] |
|---|---|---|
| I'm pleased the door is open this time. I wonder what I will find. Something interesting, I hope. | *"Quend en naissent la Dame que j'adore, De ses beautez vint embellier les cieux, Le fils de Rhee appella tous les Dieux Pour faire d'elle encore une Pandore."* *Huh, les hommes. Toujours le piedestal.* | An Englishman walks into an old church. Inside there is only one person, a guide. The guide is reading a book of archaic french love poetry. |
| A woman. Hmmm. What a fascinating place. Haven't got a clue, but very interesting. And this guide. Such dark hair, such a porcelain white complexion. Interesting! | *Un homme. Un homme seul. Oh merde! Un homme seul et anglais. Un peu mouille.* | The Englishman enters, looks at the guide and then speedily looks down the main aisle of the church, seeing many varied works. His gaze returns to the guide. The guide looks up from her book. |
| "Bonjour" | *"Bonjour"* | They exchange greetings. |
| "Combien?" | *"Eh bien. C'est cinq francs pour cette entree. Mais si vous voulais voir les expositions de les trois eglise, vous pouvez acheter un billet pour seulement neuf francs."* | He asks, rather commonly, for the price and she responds by stating the price and mentioning the price for the "all-in three churches festival". |
| "Oui." Oh dear. | | He smiles for some reason, yet has not quite understood. He has sufficient courage to ask again. She waits |

"Pardonne?"

Ah, that'll be interesting.
"Pour les trois, s'il vous
plait."

"Merci."

Hmmm, fascinating.
Sculptures of all kinds.
And pictures too.
And what's this, floor to
ceiling bamboo. No
English subtitles here!
"La foret ou l'oeil se
perd." Where the eye
gets lost? ".et l'individu
se trouve pris au piege
du labryinthe." Caught
in the labrynthe? And
this? An apothecary
chest of a sort?
"L'artiste est sans doute
la seule personne a
pouvior descendre en
soi-meme, a se risquer
dans son labryinthe avec
une chance de ressortir."
Something about losing
and finding yourself I
suppose and the
labryinthe again. Now
haystacks. Let's see.
"Elles forment un
labryinthe." So labrynth
is the idea perhaps!

*Er,..zere are sree churches*
*'aving exeebicion. U can*
*'av ticket for zem.. tout.*

*Monsieu"*

*Il est pal mal.*

*Plutot bien conserve pour*
*son age.*

*J'aime ses epaules.*

*Il est vraiment absorbe.*
*Moi aussi!*
*"Va, livre, va, desboucle*
*la barriere,*
*Lashe la bride, et asseure*
*ta peur,"*
*Toujours barriere, et*
*toujours la bride, et*
*toujours les peurs.*

*Je vais lui parler.*

How language unites
and divides people. She
is patient, maybe up to a
point. He is hoping he
doesn't have to ask
again.
He buys the complete
festival ticket.

He begins to look
around. She remains at
her desk.
Now, what is going on
here?
Something like a dance
is beginning.
A little disjointed.
Perhaps more like stellar
objects in orbit.

The tempo of this dance
may change. There are
ingredients of many
possibilities.

Maybe a dance. Maybe
stellar objects in
attraction.
Maybe a hunt.
[The rabbit is absorbed,

Oh. She's walking this way.
She's rather attractive.
Not very tall.

"Et. Er, peut etre. C'est les formes du labrynthe, n'est ce pas?"

Wonderful! A "bien sur."
This begins to make some sense.

She's very attractive.

"Et le minotaur. Pleins de contradictions et de possibilite, n'est ce pas?"

What a nice smile.

She's going back to her desk.
She moves well.

Now! Concentrate on the exhibition man.

*"Vous comprenez le theme, monsieur?*

*"Oui, bien sur."*
*Il ne me semble pas tres convaincu!*
*Mais peut etre qu'il s'y connait.*

*Il me regarde vraiment beaucoup!*

*"Oui."*

*En fait, il semble s'v connaitre plutot bien.*
*Sufficient.*
*Il faut que je laisse manitenant.C'est trop difficile - son francais et mon anglais.*
*Il a plutot l'aire intelligent quand il me regarde.*

*Retourner a mon livre.*

*"Je veux mourir pour tes bealitez, Maistresse ..."*

the fox trots towards.]

Maybe the dance. They connect, without quite looking at each other. Faltering steps, but they are steps of a sort.

A conversation. A conversation about one thing and about many other things too.
If they are stellar objects. Gravity begins! He is looking at her now.

The dance is best I think!
A gentle waltzing for positions.

There is some awkwardness here. This dance is enough, for now.

Now, from ballroom to latin in an instant.
He watches her walk away.

A trail of invisible string now links the pair. [A

| | | |
|---|---|---|
| | | tragic myth!] |
| Is this Icarus, and ... | *C'est mieux quand il n'y a personne ici.*<br>*"Je veux mourir pour ceste blonde tressse ..."*<br>*Toujours les blondes!* | He steals a look in her direction and returns to Icarus. [Another tragedy!] She reads. |
| She's not watching me, yet I'm becoming so aware of her presence ... | *"Je veux mourir pour le brunde ce tient ..."* | |
| It's the moment he falls into the sea..... I think. | *Vraiment, il est charmant. Un peu.* | |
| | *Il va partir.* | |
| "Et, er, ou est l'eglise prochain?"<br><br>Oh dear. | *"Suivez la route a Poitiers, et quand vous arrivez au bout, prenez la route a droit et quand vous etes au parc, tournez a gauche: l'eglise est a deux cent metres sur la gauche."* | Now we see the treading on of toes. A collision? A disaster or a natural phase?<br><br>He seems a little embarrassed. She, a little frustrated. [Patient up to a point!] |
| "Er, pardonne? Encore, s'il vous plait?"<br><br>Ooooh dear.<br><br>Oh dear, I can't ask her again! I'll leave and hope for the best. | *Ah, pourqoi demand en francais si vous ne comprenez pas la reponse!*<br>*"Bien, go on ze road to Poitiers and at ze top of ze road, turn right and, er, if you get to the green, go left and it is not far away on left.* | Yet, in a way this too maintains the connection. They simply discomfort themselves in similarly different ways. Who is to say whether this is complementary or not? She stands using her arms, and doing her best to smile.<br>He nods and smiles |

"Merci.  Merci bien."

*"Mon plaisir."*

benignly.

A farce?  If so, then with out much as much humour as there might be. The objects move apart, and the dance continues, as the ball of string unwinds.

This isn't that difficult.  I might trust myself more. Must have looked a complete ...
But I'm not a complete ...
Am I?
This is most enjoyable, after all.
Right here.
Bit of an adventure - for a man like me anyway.

*"Mais non, arreste, et demeure en ton rang, Bien que mon couer bouillame d'un beau sang,*
*... ...*

He walks, questioning every turn until he sees the second church, high on the hill.  She returns to her book, in the thick stone cool quiet church, and reads.

Minds wander apart as they physically separate. The string reels out between them.  A connection of sorts remains.

He nears the second church.

I wonder if there will be another entrancing guide

*Je me demande s'il y a aura d'autres visiteurs cet apres midi ...*

I'm looking forward to this!
Through a curtain, and ... total Blackout! No, not quite.  There are laser lights to guide my

*J'aimerai bien quitter Melle. Habiter a Madrid ou peut etre Lisbon? Je pourrais me consacrer a mon art, creer. Je will create. Lisbon, je pense.*

He enters and is absorbed by the labyrinth of his present, she contemplates a labyrinth of her future. They both consider their

movements through the otherwise sheer black labyrinth.

I prefer a human guide, especially of the female French form. Fatale? So pale! Porcelain. I wander in these "cercles concentrique" and read, "Ainsi, Immanence et Transcendance peuvent se rejoindre au coeur de chacun". Is this some sort of human condition of searching.
There is nothing more to hold me here.

To the third then. I've seen a signpost. This will be relatively easy.
Here we are.
What an amazing entrance.
Walking down to the door. And, what a door, so old.
Oh. Full of flower arranging French folk. I might look around, but,.. no, nothing to keep me here.
I want to go back and ... Hmm?

*Lisbon, c'est bien pour les ceramiques.*

*Il etait un peu comme un Monsieur Hulot anglais! Un peu triste et un peu comique.*

*Il n'y a rien pour qui me retienne a Melle.*

*Personne visite? C'est pleasant, mais un peu trop quiet.*

*Sans personne pour deranger - pas meme un anglais excentrique. Un bon moment pour penser, un bon moment pour lire. "Je veux mourir es amoureux combas, Soulant l'amour, qu'au sang je porte enclose Toute une nuit au milieu*

present mysteries and possibilities and what holds them in their lives.

The connection is still alive.

They move on.

He sees the route this time. He is the enthused traveller. For her this afternoon is so much like all others, except for this funny foreign man.

Rewind the string. To what end?
She has a certain pragmatism. He has not. He seems a little

| | | |
|---|---|---|
| Is this wise? What am I doing?<br>Do I want to?<br>Yes I do.<br>How attractive is she? | *de tes bras."*<br>*Oui, tes bras.* | ungrounded, uncertain in flight<br>Not of the earth.<br>She is earthly and earthy.<br>Earthy and strong.<br>She is in latin mode. He may lose his core if he's not careful. And more! Balance is key to the dance.<br>He walks back and into the first church. |
| Be calm not too self conscious. | *Oh mon Dieu!* | She looks up, he looks away, averting his eyes along the aisle. |
| "Bonjour, j'ai fini mon tour."<br>I will look around once more | *"Re bonjour." "Tres bien."*<br><br>*Comme c'est charmant, cet homme pas tres sur de lui.* | Now, she seems slightly amused, slightly pleased.<br><br>The string pulls tight. He looks at Icarus once more. A portent? |
| I'm looking at Icarus again. | *"J'ai fini dans cinq minutes."* | She picks her book and picks up her basket. Something will happen! Is he too close to the sun? |
| Shall I ask her if she wants to go for a drink? | | Will these stellar objects collide?<br>Will the dance take off?<br>What rhythm?<br>Will they connect? |
| I feel a little colour in my cheeks. Am I too close to the sun. | *Est ce qu'il va me proposer d'aller boire un verre? Ce serai bien.* | |
| It's now or never. Will I? | | Will he prove clueless once more? |

# Part Two

# Change Processes

# 11

# Swish!

Dear Anita,

Do excuse me for the haste of this e-mail. It's just that I've had the most amazing experience. As you know I am constantly fighting my own little battle of the big bulge and, anyway, I decided to see a therapist. I simply must tell.

My therapist and I decided it would be a good idea for me to give up chocolate biscuits. This would help me on my way to becoming "slim, trim and beautiful", which he said was my well-formed outcome. I responded by saying that "well-formed" was what I was already - it was just that I had overdone the input as opposed to the outcome. He didn't laugh. I have to admit that it had taken us about half an hour to get to "slim, trim and beautiful". When we began, you see, he kept on asking me what I wanted and I kept on saying I didn't want to be so fat and he kept on asking what would I prefer! I'm sure my therapist was ever so slightly redder in the face by the time we had got over this. He's a PNL therapist, or something like that.

Well Anita, the first thing he got me to do was to eat a chocolate biscuit, which was very nice, yet puzzling. I pointed out that I thought the idea was not to eat biscuits. He coughed slightly and then he asked me, unbelievably, to pick up another and notice what I saw just before I put the biscuit into my mouth. I felt like saying, what on earth do you think I saw! Well! I didn't need to pick up another biscuit did I? So I told him,
"The biscuit."

He asked me to "pick one up, please" so I did. He stopped me just before the biscuit entered my mouth.
"Miriam, remember this. This is your Cue picture." he announced.
"My what?" I said.

"Your Cue picture." He repeated.

"Oh! Is that queue with a "q", cue with a "c" or something to do with billiards? And, if it is queue with a "q", where am I in it?"

He did do a sort of smile this time, although it did seem a rather unhappy one if you can have such a thing. He quietly requested that I remember the image of the biscuit just before it entered my mouth. I said I would. Then he asked me one of his ever so slow and obviously ever so meaningful questions.

"And, ... Miriam, ... can I check that you are ... associated ... in this picture?"

"What?" I exclaimed, "Associated to whom or what and how?"

"I mean, are you seeing the picture of the biscuit through your own eyes?"

"Who else's would I be looking through?" I asked.

"I mean, Miriam, that this picture is of the biscuit as it would appear just before it enters your mouth, and is not a picture with you in it."

"My hand's in it." I suggested, a little sheepishly.

"That's fine." He said, a little relieved.

"Now," he went on, "I would like you to put a frame around that picture."

"Any particular type of frame?" I asked, mildly bewildered.

"Any kind you like." He replied, rather hopefully I think.

I simply nodded and said "ok".

Then, believe it or not, he asked me to forget this picture. Only after I quizzed him rather severely about why had I done all of this in the first place, if all I was going to do was forget it, did he say that I would be "using it "later. This interaction seemed to have added a definite glow to his complexion.

After a couple of deep breaths, he explained that he wanted me to create an "outcome picture". This would be a picture of me in the most desirable form that would result from me being "slim, trim and beautiful". In order to prompt this picture, he asked, how would you be and what would be happening as a result of being "slim, trim and beautiful". I didn't dare tell him about the thong and things, and when he told me to enhance the picture as fully as I could I also didn't tell him who else was in the picture and what they were doing. This was a cue [with a "c"] for another of those questions,

"And, Miriam, can I check that in this picture you are disassociated." In response to my befuddled expression, he added, "I mean, are you seeing yourself in the picture?" I was fairly sure that nodding was what he wanted me to do and since I was also sure that I was watching what was going on in this picture, I nodded.

If there had been a slightly ridiculous sense to everything so far, then the whole thing was about to become completely bizarre. He asked me to shrink this "outcome picture" down to a small black dot. I protested! I wanted to keep this picture and didn't want anything in it to shrink especially as I was now

perfectly formed. He assured me that I would not be losing the picture and that it would reappear frequently and brilliantly and powerfully. On that basis and on that basis only, I told him, I agreed to make it into a dot.

Then things became a little complex as well as bizarre. He asked me to bring back, in my mind that is, the cue picture [the chocolate biscuit] and put the dot of fabulous me attended by admirers in the bottom right hand corner of the cue picture. I showered him with questions. Why? What for? What is so significant about the bottom right hand corner? Isn't that a tad silly? Was he sure? Did he really mean that? He certainly looked drenched by the time I'd finished with him. There were little beads of perspiration on both temples. They were arranged in almost perfect symmetry and were slowly dropping down his forehead.

Anyway, eventually I did what I think he was asking me to do and had a little black dot in the bottom right hand corner of my chocolate biscuit picture. Then it happened. [It took a little time, not un-surprisingly, for him to explain in a way that made sense.] He asked me to "explode" the dot all over the chocolate biscuit picture when he said "Swish". When I was ready, he would shout "Swish" and I was to do the exploding as quickly as possible. It's to be just like the Swish of a curtain and very fast he said. Then the wonderful thong picture of me would explode all over the other one and would be all I was able to see. After doing this just two or three times, he said to me "sotto voce",
"As the cue picture comes into your mind, Miriam ... notice what happens ... now."
Amazing! I couldn't hold that chocolate biscuit picture in my mind. As soon as I thought chocolate biscuit picture ... "Swish" my beautiful thong picture would appear covering the complete landscape of my mind.

I'm not sure how to explain it, but if my mind is full of railway lines, it was as if a new set of points has been put in. The nearest suggestion of chocolate biscuit and hey presto!

He tried to give me another biscuit. I recoiled and smiled simultaneously. The desire to achieve my beautiful thong picture was so strong that I could easily reject his offer.
"What did you do that for?" I asked.
"I wanted to check how well the Swish was working." He replied.

Working or what! Ever since I haven't had a chocolate biscuit and have lost nearly a stone in two weeks. Triumph.

I am a little worried about having bought ten sets of new curtains for the house. I wonder if it has anything to do with my attraction to that swish sound? Also, I do enjoy the supermarket experience these days. Between you and me,

every time I walk past the biscuits I feel mildly propelled to seduce any man in sight. Perhaps I will have to go and see my therapist again! Actually, there is something else about supermarkets I want to discuss with him.

Yours,

Miriam

Ps - Can't wait to show you how "slim, trim and beautiful" I am. Must meet soon.

# 12

# Squash!

Dear Miriam,

I can't tell you how much happiness I have now in my life. What I can tell you is that it is all down to you, my dear Miriam. Your e-mail was an inspiration.

It seems so long ago, since you told me of your experiences with your therapist. Personally, I don't have a problem with biscuits or weight or much at all really. On reading your story, however, I was led to consider some of the disappointments in my life. I decided this would be an appropriate time to face them. Your therapist seemed to be a kind and patient man, so I went to see him.

He was as you had hinted, crumpled and kind, wrinkled and wistful and so slow that there must be some depth. What I liked more than anything else was the way he attended to me. In those moments with him, it was as if there were no other thoughts, no single distraction, no conscious process, and no sense of anything except his attention to me. As you can understand, dear Miriam, this led me to express myself comfortably and fully.

I was there, I said, to find what was missing in my life and for the resolution of some seeming conflict. *As he listened to this, he raised an eyebrow and inclined his head, so I told him and this I said, ...*

*I have lived a life that is somewhat lonely, yet I think I quite like it like that. I enjoy my solitude and go my own way and there's something peaceful that slightly gets lost when others come round me and into my life. [Perhaps I live like a cat.] Yet, I would like a man and I want to be loved, I want to give reign to my passion. My body yearns for the touch of such hands that set my feelings aflame. I do so want it to happen.*

*So I told him all this and he looked at me deeply and smiled like a man in a*

*trance. He said, be just quiet, and relax yourself, while I mix up something for you. A squash, he said, an unusual mixture, yet one that I think will work well. So he took down a glass and gathered some bottles and poured a little from one. Then he took up another and added some more, this time an essence of lemon. As it went in so it merged with thick luscious orange and turned a most curious colour. After some time it seemed to just settle, intriguing and different and new. And when it was still, although not quite static, he held it for me to then drink.*
*Once I had drunk, he asked me to settle and even to close my eyes.* *

*"Hold out one hand," he asked me quite kindly, "and on it create an image. An image of you that enjoys independence and values it ever so highly."*
*Then there it was, sitting serenely. Where it came from, I'm really not sure, yet clear and sparkling, like ice white diamonds, an "I" in that old fashioned capital way. [Not a dagger, but clearly before me!] I held it so still and what truly surprised me was when I began to feel weight on my hand. Then I heard his voice, through a shimmer of mist,*
*"And of this part, this part on your hand, what is the positive intent?"*
*I answered, not really in words, though I knew it was self - reliance, control - and having my own right path. The "I" was now able to move and to sparkle, and colours began to flare out. The twinkle was gorgeous, the yellow was golden, the green and the indigo spliced and still the "I" was pristine and polished and deeper the now harder ice.*
*He asked me to lower my hand for a moment and let the image go. After that he told me to hold out the other. As soon as I had, he said,*
*"Create an image, on this hand, of that other part of you - whatever comes into your head."*
*My head, I thought, now there's a joke, for what stood on my hand was a heart, red and pounding, glowing and moist and certainly very intense.*
*There was no need, it seemed, for the words that asked for its positive quest. The answer was there, like a tentative echo, the intention was not so much clear as compelling, compulsion is what I could feel. The heart was no longer happy alone. It needed another to beat along side to help it to grow and develop. The pounding grew louder, the beating was faster. His voice was a welcome intrusion.*
*"And let that image go for a moment. Let it float away."*
*"You might want, Anita, to create a third image, and if you did it would be a picture of what you do most want, or a mixture of positive intents, - or not." His voice slightly faltered and then he stopped. He knew it was not what I wanted.*
*"So what I will ask you to do in a moment is to recreate each image. Recreate them at the same time, one on either hand. Then I will ask you to allow the images to somehow move into one, and once your hands are clasped, or combined, I will ask*

you to bring them into yourself, into your very heart."

"That seems to me to be quite straightforward." I had said, with the nonchalance born of innocence.

"So relax right now and first have the one image, and then the other, and then hold them both at one time. Hold them out before you."

There was I, sitting most gently. On one hand was the "Ice white "I", on the other the pounding red heart. Images, yes, but the weight was so startling!

"And now bring your hands slowly together, or quickly and only when and how you want."

For a long, long time I noticed no movement, just saw and felt my two selves. In each hand was something of me, something I truly loved. Yet in some way they had fought each other and now that would no longer do.

Then all I felt was my hands moving slowly, ever so ever so slowly together. [My body did this, not my mind.] And at one point, as the two became closer, sparkling white flakes began to cascade on the red pounding mass by its side.

Colour was crashing, crimson vermilion, red, orange, purple, like fireside shards on the hearth.

Closing my hands took great physical effort. They trembled and shook as they closed.

This was not the end, dear M, as I was soon to discover.

"Now bring your hands in to yourself, as quick or as slow as you want to."

How quickly or slowly my clasped hands moved, I admit, I really don't know. Yet move they did, towards my chest, - when my hands touched my body I felt it. A little jolt, and a tear and a tingling. I thought and said nothing for ages.

He chatted about all sorts of things before I left, shopping, cars, pavements, healthy results of walking briskly. I interrupted him and asked,
"Did it work?"

He stopped for a moment, smiled and said,
"How well, you will find out."

Oh, sorry Miriam, must go now. I'll tell you what happened soon.

Love,

Anita

*This is a metaphor! Exotic cocktails of any kind might be confined to life outside the coaching or therapy context.

# 13

# Dealing with Difficult Vegetables

Anita, how could you? I am left in complete suspense. How very exciting. I can't wait to hear what happens as a result of you being squashed. It is wonderful to have a good therapist, don't you think?

I am feeling fabulous. The success with chocolate biscuits is changing my life. My trips to the supermarket are becoming ever more frequent and enjoyable. Even when I don't buy anything, I simply enjoy walking around with my trolley. Strangely though, walking around with my trolley has led me to return to our mutual friend.

I began to realise that every time I went past the fresh vegetables, I would begin to get a queasy feeling. I decided to test my reactions. I would walk past each vegetable and look at it very intently. One of the stackers even asked me if the broccoli was bothering me. Anyway, potatoes, parsnips and peas were passable. Tomatoes were tolerable and although I have never been keen on beetroot, it too passed without any particular sense of unease. Despite my special regard for celery, I checked it and the other anaemics - lettuce, leeks, spring onions and squash - and they all allowed easy passage [no pun intended]. Then I realised. There they were in front of me, and as I stood motionless before them, so the "queasiness" increased. It was the radishes. I can hardly bear to write the word, or think of them.

So I rang and said I needed to see him. I want you to cure my phobia, I said. He seemed a little hesitant.
"You can do it, can't you?" I asked.
"Yes" he said, "although we don't actually use the term phobia cure, because you can never be sure."
"What never?" I said. There was a second hesitation on the other end of the line.

"Never be sure of what?" I continued.

"Well, that it is actually a cure."

"But you can do it, can't you?"

"Yes, of course. When would you like to come and see me, Miriam?" he asked.

He sat in the same chair as before, in more or less the same way as before with what appeared to be a slightly weak smile.

"So," he began, "what is it that leads to this unwanted reaction?"

"What? Oh, it's radishes."

He sat there for a moment or two, breathing it seemed to me rather deeply. I noticed a little movement of his left hand. He was pinching two of his fingers together.

"So, if you think of radishes now, what happens?"

"I don't want to!" I said.

"O ... Kay ..., say the word again then."

As I said radishes, he looked at me very closely.

"I suppose you think that's funny." I said.

"Hmmm?"

"You can probably see me going red and beginning to sweat, even as I say it."

He said he was just testing the strength of my reaction. He smiled most sweetly as he spoke.

"And, Miriam?" cue for one of those questions I thought, "Was there a time in your past, a specific experience perhaps, which you believe leads you to have this reaction?"

"I think so." I said.

"Tell me about it Miriam, if you can."

I explained that I was very young at the time, about five I think. My mother had encouraged me towards culinary expertise from an early age. She would show me how to prepare salad and as soon as I was able to use the kitchen knives safely, she had demonstrated how to "chop, chop, chop" the various vegetables. Tomatoes, lettuce, cucumber, and even onions were all "chop, chop, chopped" until they were reduced to slim slices or small chunks. The onions, I told him, had been a little troublesome. They made me cry. They made me cry even after my mother told me to put a fork in my mouth. Mummy later explained that I should have been biting the fork landscape with either end of the fork sticking out of my mouth. This would have been rather better than trying to place it in my mouth whole and in portrait. No wonder I was still crying. I did tell her that the instruction "put a fork in your mouth" left a lot to be desired and too much to be imagined.

My mother's enthusiasm for the kitchen was matched by my father's love

of the garden. He would spend hour after hour caring for his vegetable plot. He would pop into the greenhouse to pot his seedlings and tend his tomatoes and he would spend hours in the garden shed doing I don't know what.

Anyway, one morning I got up bright and early and went to the kitchen. Mummy and Daddy were still in bed. I walked into the kitchen and there they were. Lying on the kitchen table were the largest, reddest and most beautiful radishes I had ever seen. I was helpless. I picked up a knife and in a wave of delight began to "chop, chop, chop ... chop, chop, chop." In my delight, I had obviously been singing because my father came down the stairs calling,
"Miriam, Miriam, do be quiet, it's half past four in the mor.."
His head peered round the door,
"Miriam, Miriam, Miriam!" He exclaimed. Having reached full volume, the rising crescendo stopped. After a few seconds in which he grew redder and redder [perhaps that is why I don't particularly like beetroot] he continued.....
"You stupid, stupid, stupid [the word was repeated rather a lot, I think] girl."
He picked up what was left of the bunch. Brandishing them at me, he shouted,
"These were my beautiful radishes! They were about to win prizes! Certain to win prizes! Destined to be the best radishes in Radley!"
He continued shaking the remains of the radish at me for some time. He didn't say a lot. It was more a case of foaming at the mouth, jumping up and down, and if there were words, they were something like,
"Just ... like ... your ... mother." Somewhat staccato as I remember.
I can see it now, all that brandished radish.

After I told him all this, our therapist asked if I would like some water. I said no. He said he needed a little, so would I mind if he popped out to the kitchen for a minute. He came back with a glass of water and sat down.
"Hmmm," he began, once he had completed a little finger clenching. "So if we could change that initial experience and your response to.."
"You can't change the experience." I said.
"I mean, change the way you think about the experience, so that you are no longer reddened or rattled by radish. Would that be good?"
"Oh yes. Anything. What do you suggest?"
"Well, what I'm thinking Miriam, is that we might go to the cinema.."
"Oh, lovely. When?"
"A cinema in your mind, that is." He replied.
I was quite disappointed at that. I would have enjoyed going to the cinema.
"And we will create a new version of what happened and change your response to radishes."

"Great."

"So, would you like to go to your favourite cinema, or would you prefer to create an imaginary one?"

This took me some time. I went through most of the multiplexes I knew and decided they were a little like shoeboxes.

So I decided to make one up. As I had been quiet for a few minutes, I told him,

"I'm creating my own imaginary one. I've got boxes, balconies, and royal red furnishings, but I'm having trouble with the wallpaper and the chandeliers."

His eyes widened a little, his eyebrows lifted a little and he nodded encouragingly as he pressed his fingers together.

Finally I said, "Done."

"Now, Miriam, what I would like you to do is to go and sit in that cinema. That's right. And now, on the screen in front of you, I would like you to create the original scene. A still frame, stopped at the precise moment before the action began."

"Do you think it should start before Daddy got out of bed or when he was coming down the stairs or when he poked his head around the door?"

He paused for a moment, as usual.

"What do you think, Miriam?"

"But I asked you." I said, almost stamping my foot. "I suppose when he appeared at the door."

"Hmmm." He nodded. "So have that picture now." He was looking at me very closely. "And if you want to make it a black and white picture."

"No, I prefer colour."

"And now Miriam, I am going to ask you go to a projection booth high up in the back of the cinema, and from there I want you to watch yourself watching that frozen frame picture."

I turned towards him and looked him in the eye. I might have placed a soupcon of incredulity into my look.

"You want me to do what?"

He didn't flinch. He did, I thought, become even more immobile, except for his finger twitch.

"I'd like you, Miriam, to view the scene, in your mind's eye, from the projection booth, watching yourself sitting in the stalls, and ..."

"Circle." I said.

"Watching yourself sitting in the circle, watching the freeze frame picture."

It took me a little time. After all, the first time I went to the projection booth I got a bit lost, and then when I finally found it there was no me sitting in the circle. I told him this. His response was to ask me if I was perhaps sitting in the

stalls. I gave him a bit of a look but his suggestion did have the desired effect of me creating myself sitting in the circle.

"I can see myself now." I said.

"Great. What I'm going to ask you to do now is to run the film in fast forward mode, all the way through to the end of the episode - to the time when the interaction with your father is finished and you are completely alright again. Then freeze frame the film once again."

"Like a video?"

"Exactly Miriam." He seemed so pleased as he said this. It was as if something he was dreading hadn't happened.

"Do it now."

I did and I giggled a little. It was amazing and quite funny. It stopped the movie after Mummy came down and comforted me and I was feeling fine.

"And now, I'd like you to rewind the video as fast as you can, right back to the original freeze frame, then stop."

What fun. I enjoyed this so much and once more I giggled a little.

"I'm wondering, Miriam, what would make the film even funnier? Perhaps you could have your father wearing strange clothes."

"He wasn't wearing any clothes." I replied, rather curtly.

"Hmmm. So what could we dress him in?" He continued, his fingers pressing together very strongly.

"What about pink frilly things and a nappy?"

He nodded and smiled. And after a little pause he said,

"And if I said the word elephant, would that help?"

"Oooh, yes." I said, instinctively.

"And if there were to be mirthful music or sounds accompanying the video, what would the music be?"

"William Tell." I said, also instinctively.

Oh Anita, I was getting so excited.

"Okay, so now let's have pink, frilly, nappy and elephant with William Tell about to begin and ... start that fast forward movie ... now.

Anita, I laughed and laughed and laughed so much. There was my father, sort of, with a flailing trunk, tail, and great big ears [African definitely], jumping up and down in manic accompaniment to the final crescendo of the William Tell Overture. His final leap into a splattered prone position, with radishes squeezing out from under his ample girth left me in speechless mirth. It was a shame it had to stop. When he asked me if I wanted to run it backwards again, I said

"There's no need." I knew instantly and certainly. My memory of the occasion and my reaction to it were now changed forever. Remarkable.

"So, now Miriam, if I were to ask you to be that Miriam, the one you have just

watched, but be in the screen, in the action as it were, how would you react?"
"That would be great fun." I replied.
"So, now Miriam, could I ask you to leave the cinema."
"Don't really want to." I said.
"And if I were to say "radish" to you?"
I giggled.
"And if I were to show you this?" Anita it was amazing. He produced a radish from nowhere.
"Do you always carry radish with you. Or does everybody that comes to see you find radish disturbing?"
"Not very many." He replied, whilst his fingers did that pressing movement again.
I was so pleased. I told him there and then. For the first time I saw a different smile. There was a twinkle in his eye. It was as if he was genuinely happy.
"I'm getting rather good at this visualising, aren't I?"
"Yes Miriam, you are. It is a prerequisite for genius you know."
Anita, imagine. Me, a genius.
It had taken rather a long time. Almost two hours. Just like the real cinema, I thought. It was probably designing my own cinema and then getting lost going to the projection booth that took so long. Still I didn't miss anything, did I?
As I was about to leave I asked him what he was doing with his fingers. He was a little embarrassed I think.
I thought he said he was angering himself, so I asked,
"Why would you want to be angry?"
"No, anchoring," he said. "So that I can be relaxed, alert and attentive."
"Is that difficult?" I asked.
"Sometimes." He said.

Ever since, my trips to the supermarket have become even more enjoyable. I get the giggles every time I go past vegetables and I'm just waiting for a stacker to ask me what is so amusing about an artichoke or something.
        You know, Anita, I feel I have the capability to take control of my life and enjoy living. Must go now. I'm off to Regent's Park Zoo. Let me know how you are getting on squashwise.

Love

Miriam.

# 14

# Six Steps and a Story

Oh Miriam,
It was truly lovely to receive your recent e-mail. Like me, it seems you are experiencing change and enjoying life so much.

    After being "squashed" as you put it, things did seem to be different. All of a sudden, men came out of the woodwork, a little like number seven buses. I wondered if the world had altered, or whether it was simply my perception.

    I began to notice men that I liked and even ended up talking to a few of them. During these conversations there would inevitably be a point at which one of us might mention meeting again at sometime in the future. Whenever this moment or the likelihood of this moment approached, I would freeze. It was odd and very discomforting. Either I would begin to talk nonsense, go red and feel very, very silly, or I would make some excuse to remove myself from the conversation. On one occasion, I even ended up saying "no" when I would have liked to say "yes". And so, dear Miriam, as you can guess, I went to see our kind and patient friend.

*As I told him all this, he looked and he nodded, in a way which suggested he knew. And then, he said quietly and ever so gently, I think I know what we will do.*
*He said, relax deeply, and said it again and that's all I seem to remember. Till ...,*
*"Anita" he said, "Can you go deep inside and contact that part of you? The part that controls this reaction."*
*And somewhere inside me something emerged as he asked it to give me a signal. My shoulder twitched. He said, please make it welcome, and thank it for speaking to you. And if you might ask it ever so gently,*
*"What are you there to do?"*

It was as if then I had a strange vision, a child peeping round a stair corner. Ever so shy, and ever so me, I heard a pipsqueak voice say,
"Wouldn't want to be harmed, wouldn't want to be hurt. I must, I must be safe."
I could feel a trickle. One single line of dew trickling down one cheek. I knew that young girl so well.
"Anita, I'd like you to ask this part if it will accept new behaviour. If it will condone a new way of acting that keeps the intent intact.
Will it do that for you?
Will it do that Anita?
Will it let new choices come in?"
My shoulder twitched rather quickly. It certainly said, yes, yes, yes.
"So thank it Anita, thank it quite dearly, it wants just the best for you."
"Now Anita, I'd like you to access that part, that part of you that's creative."
And at that moment another strange vision came clearly into my head. There was I in a huge great hall. From one of the boxes a face appeared and said,
"'Ello, I am Salvadora and I come from [a] somewhere in [a] Spayne."
"Oh!"
"And what can I do for [a] you?"
"Is it there Anita? Has it made itself known? Then thank it and say hello.
I want you to ask it, if it would be so kind as to give you three new choices. New ways of being in that situation that keep intact the intent."
When Salvadora had listened to this, she smiled and quietly said,
"Well, dear Anita, we can do that for [a] you. It is ever so, ever so simple." Her dark hair shook, her wild eyes sparkled, her red mouth opened wide.
"One is to question.
One is to look.
One is simply to laugh. Ha! Ha!
You want [a] some more? You have many options. I'm sure more will come to your mind."
And in a flash she had gone.
"Now, I'd like you to ask the original part, that drove the old behaviour, if it will accept the new ways of being and will own their implementation, implementing them at appropriate times, appropriate times for you."
My mind seemed so still, the vision had gone. I was totally quiet inside, and after a minute of deep relaxation, my shoulder began to twitch. It twitched in a way that encouraged a laugh. I knew it was there to say "yes".
The deep relaxation, the sense of silence, the heavy calm warmth in my limbs, let me stay in the quiet and allowed me to settle.
It was some time later he said,
I'd like, Anita, to tell you a story. I think it went something like this ...

*Her name was Magella, a would-be explorer. She went to a foreign land. Once there she chose to walk in a forest, all green and dark and intense. She wandered a while and came to a copse that was lighter in form than the rest.*

*And there she saw him, sat in a tree. A multicoloured wide eyed owl. She asked him his name. He said it was Keith, and she asked him what he was doing.*

*"I'm sitting here, as I have done for ages. You see, I cannot fly. It's my wings, you see, there's something wrong. They won't let me fly off this perch."*

*"Oh, Keith," she said, "I'm sure you can fly. Just swoop down and sit on my shoulder."*

*The owl almost moved for the first time in ages.*

*"I'm ever so frightened." He said.*

*"You're frightened?" she asked, and seeing his nod, "You're frightened of what?" she enquired.*

*"I'm not at all sure, I really don't know, I'm sure there was something once."*

*"Well, don't be afraid. Put your fears behind you. There's nothing to stop you now."*

*And Keith glided down and perched on her shoulder and squeezed his inscrutable eyes in glee.*

*They travelled for miles, till they came to a clearing. An ass stood there in a neat, chewed grass circle. Magella enquired of his state.*

*"I'm tethered," he said, "I have limitations. I can only go so far."*

*"That's surprising," she said, "for I see no stake and no slightest sign of a rope. Are you sure you're not an elephant?" She asked the astonished ass.*

*She told him how elephants used to be trained. She explained they'd be tied to a tether. If and when they would try to go further, they would be severely discouraged. The strange thing was, when the rope was removed, the elephant thought it still there.*

*"Gosh!" said the ass, in identity crisis, perplexion writ on his face.*

*"You're no elephant, and certainly not an ass. That I can plainly see. So to start your journey, please come with us now. Come my excellent donkey."*

*Entreated he followed and joined in their journey, Magella, the owl, and the donkey.*

*They wandered along for ages and ages, until they came to a lake.*

*The lake was not large. The trees had retreated. A stone-beach sloped to its shore. The coloured stones and attendant green trees were all stood waiting for something.*

*The travellers were still some way from the water, when a fabulous creature emerged. It stood by the lakeside and haltingly drank, as if from it's own reflection.*

*White and four legged, it had one straight long horn which spiralled out of its forehead. They saw it. It saw them. Both parties stood very still.*

*The moment the travellers took a pace forward the creature took a step back.*

*"Let me go see." Said the owl to Magella, and flew to it, little by little. The creature seemed startled but did not move back as Keith approached it with care. It simply looked. As it did so it noticed, it noticed the owl as it fluttered quite slowly, fluttered quite slowly toward her.*

*"We mean to be friends." Said Keith to the creature. "We certainly think you are lovely."*

*"You don't fly like an owl. How did you learn." The creature asked politely.*

*"Until now, I had not flown at all." Keith said.*

*"You stopped yourself then, for you obviously can. What has changed for you?"*

*Surprised by the statement, Keith quickly explained,*

*"I met someone who made a big difference."*

*He looked at her and she looked at him and then he called to the others.*

*"Move forward." He said, believing it safe.*

*The creature now stood and took no step back.*

*"Why did you move backward before?"*

*"I didn't know you or your intent, and how would I know you are friendly."*

*"Well I'm a donkey and this is Magella, the owl you've already met. Step by step we'd like to move closer, you're lovely, we want your acquaintance. If you want to be sure of our good intent, then by all means ask some more questions."*

*"Alright." said the creature, and let them move closer, after which they began a discussion.*

*The creature asked questions to know all about them and noticed and heard what they said. She looked at their eyes and saw their demeanour and watched what they did as they spoke.*

*After some time the creature seemed easy and mentioned it needed to go.*

*But before it did it stood right before them and said to them, each and all,*

*"You make a nice group with your different aspects, be sure you all pull together.*

*Now you keep exploring,*

*You walk in straight lines,*

*And you, let your wings spread out wide."*

*And with these words she turned from them slowly and started to move away.*

*"Will we see you again?" called a voice from the trio.*

*"I think it quite likely you will."*

*"I'm glad" said a voice, echoed by others, "So, when can we see you again?"*

*"Do ring." She answered, "Just give me a call, I'm the only one in the book! Unique!"*

*And this is the end of Magella's story, although she explored all the more. Keith could now fly and the donkey would journey, and the creature?*

*Who knows what such a lovely creature might do, now that she knew.*

It has been a few days since the session and I still think about the story. Miriam, why are you going to the zoo?

We must, must meet up soon,

Love

Anita

# 15

# Changing History

Dear Anita,

Do forgive me. It's been such a long time since your last e-mail. So much has happened, you wouldn't believe it. Well, you might, my dear Anita. I'm thrilled and literally buzzing. I don't know where to begin, but I will.

One day, as I was wandering around the zoo, I realised something. I phoned him immediately.

"What's up, Miriam?" he asked.

"I'd rather not say on the phone. I'd like an appointment." I replied.

"So, Miriam, what brings you here?" He said.

"I think I think I'm a bad person."

"A bad person."

"Yes, and I think that's behind everything. I was in the zoo, visiting the elephants, when ..."

"The elephants?"

"Yes, the elephants. After our last session I've been every other day, in between visits to the supermarket."

His brow contorted deeply. For the first time, he seemed truly uncomfortable. He didn't do any finger pressing. He simply looked down with a frown.

"I knew I shouldn't have mentioned elephants." He said.

"Oh, no." I said. "It was inspired. I've always loved elephants."

He seemed to perk up a little at this. He changed position and said,

"So you think you think you're a bad person?"

"Yes." I said.

"And is this belief linked to a specific event in the past?"

"Yes I believe it is." I replied. "I've gone to the cinema with it but even though I giggle, it doesn't change the thought that I'm a bad person. Believing I'm a bad person means I don't deserve to be successful, or have a life, or do what I want to. You know."

"I'm impressed that you've been to the cinema with it, Miriam. If that didn't work then we might need to do something else."

He sat there for a moment.

"Come on then." I said, "What strange thing are you going to ask me to do this time?"

He sat in stillness for a moment, hands in steeple touching his lips.

"Well, Miriam, I'd like to suggest that you come over here." He gestured me across the room to a clear area, near to the door. "If your life were on a path in front of you, where would the past be and where would the future be?"

I looked at him and said, "Sometimes I think you need more help than I do." He laughed at this. In fact he laughed quite a lot as I remember.

"Well?" he asked unabashed.

The amazing thing was, Anita, I did instinctively know! I pointed to my past and then to my future.

"Miriam, before we do anything else, I'd like to check, did the incident happen before or after - "radishes"?"

I giggled.

"After."

"So, Miriam, could I ask you to step to the place that represents the present and experience the sense of - "I'm a bad person". Can you do that Miriam? And as you do that, Miriam, I'm going to touch you on the shoulder. Is that alright?"

"That would be very nice." I replied.

He coughed.

"So, Miriam, experience that sense of - "I'm a bad person" now."

He touched and held my shoulder.

"Are you angering me?"

"I hope not, Miriam. I am however, intending to an..chor that feeling.

And now that you have that sense, let's go back in time, noticing all the places and times when this sense had impact in your life."

"All the places?"

"Hmmm, maybe just the main ones, Miriam."

Anita, it took ages. I was stepping backwards and continually noticing events, decisions, interactions and all sorts of situations where this thought was affecting me. Eventually I arrived at the original experience.

"Just stand over here" he said, "and from this place look at that young Miriam in that scene." He took his hand off my shoulder.

"You mean, disassociated?"

"Yes, Miriam, exactly. Are there other people involved in this experience?"

"Yes."

"And who are they?"

"Daddy and Mrs. Hubert."

"And what is the positive intent of what they're doing?"

"Rather obvious, I think."

"Oh!" He said, and paused for a moment.

"And looking at that little girl called Miriam, what was her positive intent?"

"To find out what Daddy did for so long in the garden shed." I said.

"And is there anyone or anything else that led to formulating the belief you created?"

"Yes, there's what happened that evening."

"And are there others involved?"

"Yes. Mummy and Daddy this time."

"And, as you observe this later scene, what is the positive intent of your father?"

"Survival."

"Survival?"

"Yes. He's running out of the door, with one hand removing the kitchen knife from where it lodged in his trouser belt and the other hand holding his head."

"I see. And what was the positive intent of your mother?"

"Do you mean as she stood there when he ran out of the door, or just before when she hit him with the Le Creuset and threw the knife at him as he began his exit?"

"Just generally, Miriam."

"Something about releasing anger and communicating it to Daddy at the same time, I should think."

"And what of that young girl?"

"She is concerned about the response to the question she had just put to her father."

"Which was?"

"Daddy, what exactly were you and Mrs. Hubert doing in the garden shed?"

"Miriam, what was her positive intent of that young girl?"

"Curiosity. She wanted to understand something that was confusing her."

"Is there any other experience that led her to create the belief she developed at that time?"

"She saw the resulting separation and the divorce as something she caused. That added weight to the belief that had begun."

He thanked me and moved me to the area of my present and asked,

"Looking at that present Miriam, what is a resource, competency or skill she has

now which would be useful to that young Miriam?"

"A mature perspective." I responded.

He coughed.

"So, Miriam, step into that present space and as you do, get into that sense of - mature perspective - right now. Are you doing that? Amplify and intensify that sense if you will, Miriam. And I'd like to touch you on the shoulder again. Is that o.k.?"

"Please do."

"And now, let's go back to those incidents and give that resource of mature perspective to the young Miriam, there, now."

I did it Anita. I stood there and as I watched that young girl, I gave her mature perspective.

"And now Miriam, be that young Miriam once more, witnessing those scenes, now with that added resource, the resource of mature perspective."

I was.

"Notice how your perception and response is changed. Notice how your thinking now changes as a result. Notice new conclusions."

I nodded and nodded and nodded, quite a lot I think, and then I said,

"It isn't logical to come to those conclusions is it?"

"Which ones?"

"That I caused their divorce, that I am a bad person, and all the rest."

"It's very rarely a matter of logic, Miriam. It tends to be what makes sense to a person at the time and more often than not, it has little to do with logic. Often logic is confused with coincidence or more likely "co-incidence". What are the more useful beliefs that young Miriam might come to now as you witness these scenes?"

"It must be dreadfully uncomfortable in the garden shed."

He coughed.

"Other people are responsible for their own actions and their own choices."

"And what about you, young Miriam? What conclusions might you come to?"

"I am a natural and lovely girl."

"Anything else?"

"Le Creuset is very heavy and needs to be wielded carefully. Daddy has had a scar on his head ever since."

"So, Miriam, maintaining that sense of mature perspective, let us move once more to the present and as you do, notice how the new belief about you, Miriam matures in itself as you move to the present. Notice how many of those experiences in the past are now changed and changing in your mind."

Oh, Anita, it did take a long time to get back to the present. Once there, he asked,

"Miriam, what has happened to that belief that you once had?"

"Exactly that" I said. "It was a belief I used to have. It seems far away and long ago, like Wind in the Willows."

"And how does that feel for you Miriam to have made that belief into something you used to have?"

"Very nice, thank you." I replied.

After a few moments, he said,

"Miriam, if I asked you to choose one or several new beliefs about yourself right now, what would they be?"

I took some time to answer this. I had the sense that beliefs about Le Creuset was not what he was after and it did occur to me that beliefs about Le Creuset was not what I was after either. Rather mature of me, I reflected.

"I deserve to live a happy life. I can choose to live the life I want. I am a unique and lovely and capable person."

I sort of expected a cough at this point, yet there was none.

"So Miriam, could I ask you to have the sense of - I deserve to live a happy life - right now. Miriam, shall I....."

"Yes please."

"So now that you have the sense of you deserve to live a happy life, Miriam, allow yourself to experience that sense fully. As you do, add to it the knowledge and full belief that - I can choose the life I want - you can do that, Miriam, and do it now, and notice how that adds to the sense you have and how positive you feel about yourself now. Now, I'd like you to add the sense of - I am a unique and lovely and capable person. Do that now Miriam, in your own unique and lovely way."

That made me smile.

"And notice how good these new beliefs feel and what they enable within you."

Anita, it was wonderful. I am not sure I had ever felt so positive and confident. I was suddenly and certainly confident about what I could do and what I could achieve. I stood there for about 5 minutes with tears beginning to run down my cheeks. He was still holding my shoulder, when he quietly said,

"Radishes." I giggled. "And Miriam, can I just check. You are you alright, aren't you?"

"Oh yes." I said.

"So now let us walk into the future, with those new beliefs. As you do, notice how your life is and how much you are enjoying life as you choose the life you want and experience yourself as that unique and lovely person."

As we did, my future seemed to be stretching out further and further. We walked a little. Luckily he could open the door as I continued to walk forward and explore my future. We crossed the road. He was holding my shoulder with one

93

hand and directing the traffic with the other. I can't say I was particularly bothered, but he seemed very pleased when I eventually stopped. I had been standing still for some time, when I asked him,

"Would you like to know where I am and what I am doing?"

"If you would like to tell me."

"I'm in a foreign land, embracing a large trunk and I'm very, very happy."

He looked a little bemused. I offered no further detail.

"Shall we go back now?" He asked. It was something of a plea, I think.

"So, now we are back Miriam. Knowing what you know now and knowing you deserve to live the life you want, is there anything else we need to do?"

"I don't think so."

"I will say you're good at perceptual positioning." He said.

"What?"

"I mean, you have the ability to take multiple perspectives on a situation and put yourself in other peoples' shoes."

"Thank you. Is that another part of being a genius?"

"Yes, Miriam, it is another prerequisite."

"Could I ask you something?"

"Of course."

"Do you think it would be silly of me to go to Kenya and work with the baby elephants?"

"No, Miriam, not if that is what you want to do."

"Yet it would be silly if I never ate another chocolate biscuit wouldn't it?"

"Possibly."

"And chocolate biscuits and even radishes were probably all about how I felt about myself, weren't they?"

"Probably."

"Thank you" I said.

"So, are you going to do it, Miriam?"

After a moment or two, I said,

"Probably."

He really, really smiled.

"Goodbye, Miriam."

I think he wanted to hug me, but he didn't.

So, here I am Anita. I've been in Nairobi for two months now, working at the elephant orphanage. I'm only working in the office at present, but they do say I might be able to get more involved soon and they do let me go and hug the babies [and their trunks] now and again.

I don't know when, or even if, I'll be back.

Love to you, dear Anita,

Miriam.

# 16

# The Generative Effect

Miriam,

How splendid. I was so pleased to see an email from you and to read your news. I had been a little worried that you might have been whisked off by a supermarket stacker or caged in some far away zoo! Your wonderful news reminded me that I haven't told you of my last session with our mutual friend.

After my previous session with him, especially when I stopped thinking about it and relaxed, I found myself enjoying the company of several men. I did what people used to call "dating". For me it was simply a matter of going out and having a pleasant, enjoyable time. Like you, I came to the conclusion that I could live my life in the way I wanted, and that I could, and do, create my own path. Given this sense of self determination and purpose, I rang him up and said,

*"I'm enjoying life and all's going well. I'd like to see you, just for a chat"*
*"That's fine," He said," I might not charge you for that."*
*So I went to see him, really to thank him, and when I sat down he said,*
*"Anita, how pleasing, I'm really so glad at what is happening for you. There is however, something quite different, that I'd like to offer to do.*
*You have a resource, a belief in yourself, that is worth compounding and building. And what I suggest will enhance all your life."*
*After that I took little persuading.*
*He invited me over to that special space, where you had gone through time. Yet now it was covered with sticky white tape in the form of square boxes - nine.*
*"This axis" he said "is past, present, future and this one, varied perspectives. One is for you, one for a friend and one for a guardian angel.*
*What we will do is explore all of these so your resource gets richer and stronger.*

*Would you like that, Anita? Would that be good? You can move on further and faster.*

*So first, Anita, I ask of you that you access that state and tell me some words that express it."*

I thought for a while and found many answers, and finally settled on this,

"I am now highly pleasing to myself, in life, and in the company of others."

"So access that now, and notice sensations and notice the physical feelings. Notice how strong those senses are, and notice exact location. Put your hand on the place that might be the centre and know that particular breathing. Notice your stance and the way that you are. This all makes it stronger and richer. See what you see, hear what you hear, get to know those feelings fully. That's right."

The place I held was all round my belly, around, above and below. I can feel it now, it now is so strong, I know it's there all the time.

"Now, holding that place, go into first person - that's you Anita - and go there in the present. That's right."

I did and stood there ever so still, my right hand held firm on the place.

"And where, dear Anita, would you like to go now? To self in the past or self in the future, or maybe to one of your friends. And sooner or later you'll want to go and visit your guardian angels?"

"What might be my guardian angels?"

"They're mentors, guides, imaginary spirits that care for your life from outside. They can change through time, and may not be human, it's really up to you."

I said I'd go back to myself in the past and he told me

"Keep hold of the place as you go. Looking from past to where you are now, what message do you want to offer?"

"Offer?"

"Offer or give, give to yourself, give to that present Anita. That's right."

I stood and thought, and thought for some time. Then from my past I said,

"Your life has led you up to this point, you're ready to stride ahead now."

"Now, go back to the present, go back to first, still holding the place that's so special. Now, receive the message, the message you sent from that past Anita. Notice enrichment of your sensations and notice how the strength builds, as you take this gift from the past. That's right."

And so it did. The sense truly deepened, and coursed throughout my body.

So it went on. It took us some time, as we went through all the positions. I chose several friends, you being one, to offer their gifts of enhancement. As for the angels, I chose only two and I fancy you know who one was. It caused him to cough in his self conscious way, so I later took another. This was no person, but it was the first time I have used my well-known familiar. Black, yellow eyed and ever so lithe, I'd not used her like that before.

*And from every aspect the sense would get stronger, building all through my body. I grew, and was calm, and smiled from the inside. I was really floating on air. When I had travelled the nine different stations, I thought we might finish there. Then to my surprise, we had not finished. He looked at me deeply, and said, "Dear Anita, stay in the present and listen to what has been offered. That's right."*

*He walked all around me, saying these words. I can still see-hear-feel them now,*

> *"Your life has led you up to this point, you're ready to stride ahead,*
> *Always, you were so special.*
> *You are gifted - ever and now*
> *This is so, so right for you.*
> *Anita, you're lovely,*
> *Be happy, go forward,*
> *Anita, I truly love you.*
> *Now, you sparkle coalescence, fire-coals burning brightly."*

*Since that time, the feeling's within me, yet I rarely think on it now. I'm simply more whole, and as life moves forward, what I wish for comes into my world. I remember saying, all that time ago, when you told me of chocolate biscuits, that I didn't have much of a problem. I realise now, that's hardly the point, not required for a meaningful journey. It seems to me worthwhile to look where you will, for a little, personal, development. When I left he held me, just for a moment, and we said a quiet goodbye.*

*I now have someone, someone in my life. It's very, very exciting. Whatever happens, I know I'll be fine, and that simply adds to the spice. Perhaps we could see you, out in Nairobi, as soon as we find the time.*

*Much love,*

# Part Three

# Language

# 17

# The Deletion Rap

One of the better ones.
Creations, that is.
So they say.

# 18

# The General Lies Rap

La ... La ... La ... La
La ... La ... La ...La

All these raps
Are completely the same,
None are different
Identical refrain,
In always this metre
Every time
Each one copies
And there's only one rhyme.
Everybody hates it
But no one objects
'Cos everyone likes
The universal effect.
It's a quantifier
That goes all the way,
Never doubt they're all lies
Every single day.


I can't work it out
I simply can't see
Whenever I diminish
Possibility.
I'll say I'm not able

Which is rarely true
Yet sometimes I believe it,
Is that ever true of you?
This doubting myself
I do really well
I even used to think
I couldn't spell
Witch is cleerly silley
Two beleave of me
It's meye model operater
O'ppose ability.

Now you gotta' have rules
If you're gonna succeed
Must live by them
That's the perfect creed.
Have to do it right
That has to be true,
You shouldn't do that,
I mustn't, do you?
The clear results
Which should be seen
Is to hem yourself
In someone else's dream.
That's gotta be right
To get rid of choice,
Then you needn't bother
To find your own voice.
That's the consequence
Which you now should see
Of running your life
By necessity.

# 19

# The Distortion Rap

La ... La ... La ... La
La ... La ... La ...La

If I've got this right
Then as you read this
You're experiencing,
Ecstatic bliss.
You're enthusiastic,
You want to learn.
Your intellectual drive
Is in, hyper-burn.
So, undoubtedly
I can read your mind,
It's ever so simple,
[don't mean to be unkind]
Yet when I'm on form,
When I'm - speeding,
I get pretty good at
Mind reading.
But if my form is off and I
Project illusion,
I lose rapport, and get
Confusion.
So take great care
If you think you know
Ask a question

And the seed may grow,
Then if you are right
"How do you know?"
Or "What's your evidence"
Are words that won't show.

NLP's a good thing,
Don't ask me how I know,
It's right to be inquiring
If you want to grow,
But please don't ask questions
About what I think,
'Cos the non-existent basis
Might drain out of the sink,
And leave me realising
My beliefs are uncouth,
-Illusory conjecture-
That's the truth.
So
NLP is a good thing,
Development's right,
Discrimination's wrong,
Like day follows night.
Police keep the law,
So they say,
Judges are right,
Horses say "neigh".
When you consider
What's sound and awry,
Remember -
Judgement's often -
A dubious lie.
I forgot who said that,-
Some reformer,
Or maybe an actor,
A lost performer.

Now what it all means
I really can't say
'Cos we make that stuff up,

So they say.
What it signifies,
What it really might be,
Is another conjecture,
Don't you see?
To achieve understanding
Which we ain't got yet,
Consider possibilities
As you self-reflect,
That the meaning you make-
Which can be very complex-
Is resulting of,
An equi-valence,
That you create in yourself,
To explain, in some way,
What you saw or felt
On a particular day,
Which had no meaning in the world at all,
Except the one you made,
From your meaning hall.
By which I mean,
In simpler terrain,
Meaning's what you make it,
Inside your brain.

And,
Cause and Effect
Goes a similar way,
An apple falls,
That's gravit `e,
It gives you a reason,
A truly just cause,
To go to war,
Or why someone snores,
And it helps us feel clever,
It helps to control
Minute pieces
Of the universal whole,
But it's never sufficient
And often ain't true

'Cos it's based on the limit
Within me and you.
As Einstein might say,
If he were with me,
Light's really bent,
Not A to B.

It's the same with all matters,
It's absolutely complete,
'Cos ...
We distort,-
We general lies,-
And we ever delete.

# 20

# Gaunt John Met A Model

It was a chill January night and I was walking down a narrow, tarmac pathway in a small country town. I could only guess at what this modern surface covered. Beneath it undoubtedly laid history and experience long past. I could probably dig up the street and find all sorts of artefacts and interesting construction methods. Then, I could attribute understanding and meaning to what I might find. Tarmac, mind you, can be sticky, hard and obstructive! I would, however, only dig if there were some point in digging. As long as such a search would yield new and improved understanding of an event, or a person, or the world, then it would be worth the effort. If it were so then I might even enjoy the experience and find it no effort at all.

I turned through a doorway and entered the wooden floored bar, it's comforting log fire spreading warmth on this cold, cold night. Sitting in one corner was John. John was looking down into his beer with a strained, self-absorbed expression that suggested he was seeing something entirely different from his beer! As to what was in or on his mind, that was to be discovered. Whatever lay behind that face looked deep, or troublesome, or both.

We exchanged informal formalities and I sat down beside him with my large glass of red wine.

"Well?" I enquired, with artful vagueness.

"I met a model," said John sadly, his tanned face rather gaunt under the slightly silver bristles of his sparse beard.

"What model specifically?" I asked.

"Claudia" he replied, shiftily.

"How did you meet her?"

"I was asked to interview her for a magazine."

"Which magazine?"

"No, Models of the World". He replied all too literally.

"And what sort of model was she, specifically?"

"One that caused me some confusion."

"Oh, how specifically did this model cause you to choose confusion?" I asked, going for just one of my options. Something of a frown crossed his brow before he replied,

"Well, she sends out messages that cause misunderstanding!"

"Hmmm, how exactly have you been misunderstanding the model?" I chose. The slightest glare was added to his frown.

"It's just that she doesn't show me whether she likes me or not?"

"It's "just that" is it? So, tell me John, what is most important to you, whether she shows you she likes you, or whether she actually likes you?"

"You're confusing me!"

"So, John, this is the second time you have given others the credit for creating confusion in you. Let me ask you, how specifically did you make yourself confused by the model?"

"Could you cut out the specifically please!" was his curt reply.

"Okay...." Someone on the course had mentioned that too much "specifically" might lead to some negativity!

"So, let me ask you, John, what needs to happen for you to acknowledge yourself as the creator of your own confusion?"

"You're trying to upset me, aren't you!" This reaction had also been mentioned as a possibility. Perhaps I had been a little purist in my questioning.

"What is it in the way I am behaving that encourages you to think I would be trying to do such a thing?" I chose, resisting the temptation to go for another attribution of causality.

"Well, your questions are rather odd, none too sympathetic, and don't make much sense. Or as you would probably prefer me to say, I can't make any sense of your questions!" I was pleased at his rephrasing and resolved to be more sympathetic and straightforward.

"Hmmm, okay. So, let's get back to Claudia. What did you want to find out from her?" I asked, giving him the option, so I thought, to interpret as he wished.

"That's better," he said.

I resisted the temptation to ask "better than what?" and "how specifically was it better?" on the basis of maintaining what remains of my facial features and in the spirit of rebuilding rapport!

He continued,

"I was asked to write one of those profile pages, you know, where you find out about a passion, a fear, and all that stuff."

"Yeah," I responded, with interest and enthusiasm. "How did it go?"

"I asked her about a passion she had and she gave a strange answer!" said John. "She said that she did not have a passion at all, but rather she "passioned"! When I gave what might have been a look of confusion, she added that she was passionate about many things in a whole hearted, strong feeling sort of way. She went on to say that she was passionate about her work and her career. She was in fact, so passionate that she would not do anything that might endanger, limit or foreshorten her working life! These models do say strange things!"

"What, all models?"

"Well, maybe not all models, but to say she "passioned"! It is so important to use proper English, isn't it?"

"Who says?" As the words came out of my lips, I sensed a reaction from John that encouraged me to ask a second question without waiting for a reply.

"I mean, who is using English properly important to?"

"To me" he said, as if he was stating the obvious.

"And what is important to her?" I asked, wanting to change tack quickly.

After a thoughtful pause, he replied,

"Her work and her career"

"And, what did she fear?" I enquired

"It's funny you should ask that. When I asked her if she had a fear, she answered like she had when I asked her about a passion. She said that she didn't have a fear, but rather she feared one or two things. Especially she feared getting wrinkles. She feared wrinkles so much that she had an aversion to looking into a mirror on the basis of fearing to see a wrinkle. I said that it was strange for her to choose to react to her own face in that way, when I would just notice how lovely it was!"

"Hmmm", I nodded, "and how did she respond to that, John?"

"Well, she seemed to giggle, yet it was an inside sort of giggle. It was like a saucepan full of boiling water with a lid on! Such a strange woman!

"Strange compared to who or what," I asked.

In response to the ensuing glare, I continued,

"In what way was she strange, John?"

The glare continued. I think, once again, he thought I was deliberately annoying him. [If you are an archaeologist, then you do need to dig carefully or you might damage some of the treasures.]

Eventually he continued,

"I can't work it out."

In deciding not to go for the likely lie about his capability, I responded more easily with,

"Can't work out what?"

"How she felt about me."

"What is stopping you working it out?" I queried, returning to the likely lie.

"Well, on the one hand she seemed to like me and on the other hand she didn't."

I was tempted to ask not only how he had managed to get the lovely Claudia to sit on his hands, but also how he had managed to get her to sit on one after the other. I didn't. I simply asked,

"What did she do or not do that encouraged you to think that she disliked you?"

"She never smiled at me."

"Never?"

"Well, hardly ever! And if she almost did it was in that pot boiling sort of way."

"So, John, let me ask you this... how does her not smiling at you mean that she doesn't like you?"

"Well, if people don't smile at you, then they don't like you!"

"What leads you to believe that?" As I watched his slight frown, I allowed a few moments of silence, then added,

"John, has there not been one occasion when someone that you know likes you has not smiled at you, or when you have not smiled at someone you like?"

There was another pause during which John's expression lifted a little.

"I guess so." Said John, a little hesitantly. I continued,

"What else could her not smiling at you mean?" I watched him while his eyes began to roll, the telltale sign of an internal, transderivational search for information, for meaning and new possibilities. When he seemed to resettle, I added,

"John, what would be a possible positive intention of hers in only smiling in that pot with a lid on way?"

During this next pause, I was sure he began to smile. I smiled in return. After a short while he announced,

"Thank you, that's really helpful. By the way, I can tell that you like me."

"Oh, how do you know that John?"

"You're smiling." Said John triumphantly.

"Might there be another reason for my smile?" I enquired, being careful to ask gently and smile.

After a pause that was neither too long nor too short I asked,

"John, tell me, what did she do that encouraged you to think that she liked you?"

"Well, firstly, she let me interview her for much longer than I expected and then, near the end, she asked me what would have to happen for her to have another interview with me at a different time and place."

This was another time to pause.

"How did you reply John?"
"I said that I'd need to talk to my editor."
"John!" I exclaimed.
"What?" Said John.

# 21

# Embedding Richard

A man walked briskly up the steps of a Victorian town house, now converted to modern use. As he entered the doorway, he sensed the place missed a family. His supervisor, he reflected, had taken care to make her room warm, comfortable and welcoming. He stepped through the open door.

"Come in Richard, lovely to see you. Take a seat," she gestured as much as said. "How well are you today?" she continued.

He smiled and sat down.

"I'm fine thanks, Celia. You?"

"Great, just great. So, is there anything you would like us to work on today?"

He took a moment and then began,

"Well, there is one thing. I suppose it's a question of ethics. You know, about the therapist, client relationship."

"Hmmm?"

"I've got this client, a woman, and I really like her and I keep getting the temptation to put in the odd embedded command."

"Like what?"

"Err, you know, like ...,

-whether or not you enjoy this session with me, you might want to take things further, or ...

-sooner or later you will go out, with me, sitting here as you close the door,... or ...

-you don't have to enjoy my company in order to progress,...

So, you know, the sorts of things we might say anyway." He felt himself squirming slightly as he spoke.

"As your supervisor I think you are right to raise this issue. It is a matter of ethics. I think that intention is so important in these matters, don't you?"

He nodded.

"So as long as you never say anything like ... uh, ... be really attracted to me, or ..., regardless of developing a deep attachment to me ... You are probably alright.

Anyway, it seems to me, Richard, that it would be wiser to pass her over, as a client and, thinking about what I've just said, you might want to set your relationship intentions elsewhere. As I say, it seems that way, to me, Richard."

"Hmmm. Yes" He said thoughtfully. "I suppose it would be best. Is this a common issue?"

"It is." She replied. "My own supervisor would say to me....

As you work with your clients, try to resist the thought,.. be interested in me.. and all will be well. Not that I ever had a problem in this area."

"No, I suppose not." Richard replied. "How do you do it?"

"Richard, I say to myself, be true to me, myself that is, and then I know I am acting with positive intention."

"So as long as you are acting with good intention, you're fine?"

"I am," she replied quickly, before continuing, "So, before we go further, it would be good to bed down on this issue, don't you think?"


"Hmmm. Yes."
"Uncross your legs" she began,
"and allow your hands to rest on your thighs
and,
as you begin to relax,
and ...,
you might want to
notice your breathing
and
take a deep breath
and
notice how you relax much more
as you
let your breath go,
that's right, let go,
and
close your eyes now,
that's right,
and
be aware of feelings of warmth in your body,

as you
relax and give yourself time,
that's right,
you deserve to,
let go and relax,
that's right,
and
let go the busy thought traffic
and
relax more deeply now
because your conscious mind
can do whatever it likes
as your unconscious mind
continues to hear and
understand
what is really important ...

And ...
As you deeply relax,
you might notice that,
like me,
you will only respond to what you want to,
like me,
and then follow your desire with true intent,
just like me.
Since
of course,
you would only do what was ethical with your clients,

like me,
because you would
resist the temptation to say ...
You would like to ask me out tonight,
or
I can tell you are becoming attracted to me..
As,
like me,
you wouldn't want to
do that,
would you Richard?

So,
you might want to
feel comfortable now
as you relax more deeply
be confident that you can ask me
anything
you might like,
And
as you make new decisions
and changes
in your life,
you might want to act on them ...
sooner or later ...,
Or today ...,
Or before the day is out..
And,
whether you want to ask me now or later,
you can,
Richard.
So,
just as easily as you open a door,
so
you can act on you choice,
like me,
just ask,
and
I remember one of Milton's favourite stories ...,

It was about a young **tomato plant, Richard**, that was growing and developing in the new and wonderful ways they do, you know. This **young plant, Richard**, had already changed from seedling to yellow flower and, how the young plant **loved the cilia**, from yellow flower to small green fruit and was becoming excited about the future and the new directions and decisions of life. Now **the plant, Richard, extremely green**, looked around for inspiration and as he did, his eyes set on a most beautiful **red** ripe tomato just **above him**. **You are lovely** said the young plant, Richard, and I hope **you can see** that **I am lovely too**.
**So keen** was the young plant, **Richard**, that he continued rather than wait for an answer and said **I want to be close to you** and grow towards you, just as the sun shines every day.
The response then came from the lovely ripe red plant, Richard, you don't have

to **love me** to grow you know. Even though you **look at me admiringly** that means you can make your own choice about how much **you love me** and that means you can grow as growth will bring you **closer to me** and that will make you happier and more fulfilled, if, as you do , you want to be ... **like me, a lot.**

And, Richard, the young plant replied, **yes, yes, yes**, and just as the sun ripens and grows so **you will grow towards me** and **like me** more and more every day, said she, indeed, whether or not you believe me I can see this happening **now** and as soon as you like you may even now know or know now that you will **take action** as easy as **when you open the door** and ask me if you're sure that is **what you want** to do next.

And the young plant, **Richard**, wanted **to touch** the full fruit and run his hands **all over her soft ripe skin**, but he couldn't tell her that, because he was a tomato plant and didn't have hands, which is why **we are so lucky**, don't you think? Anyway, the young plant seemed resolved to do whatever he would, wherever it came from and whether **he loved the full fruit** already or not, he knew **he would as do you** and I know, and it would be **soon**, anyway,

And have you ever noticed, Richard, as John used to say, or as John used to say Richard, how similar are intontion and intenation? Only a couple of letters and they are about the same, so to speak, so to say, how much do you **like me, Richard**, the intontion would be heard in the intenation as to whether or not you stressed the "**like me**" or the "how **much**", Richard, and that brings me to two other words that are so similar, or not, punctuation and punctuality,

Since you know, timing is everything and so when you **pause at the door** is important to your timing don't you think, because when you mix your punctuationality with your intenation you will **find the right time to ask** the question or say what you want to, **like me, Richard.**

And I know you would want to be clear about punction and intenality and all those subtle ways you influence your client to, **like me**, Richard, do **what you want.**

So, now it is time to allow your unconscious mind to **make some decisions** for you as your, um, conscious mind continues to relax yet slowly become more awake and as you slowly awaken and feel refreshed and more energetic and more decisive so you can enjoy the rest of the day in just the way you would like ... Now ..."

Richard opened his eyes.

"How good was that for you?"

Richard simply smiled both vaguely and certainly.

"So that seems to bring us to the conclusion of the session?"

"Yes," said Richard, seemingly incapable of any other remark.
"So, till the next time."

She stood, seeming to him taller than he had noticed before.  She held his hand for a moment.
Richard moved to the door, opened it and turned towards her, noticing her abundant red hair and her fair skin.  From somewhere inside him a question was forming,
"Celia, would you like to ...

# 22

# La Musee
## [Guide map available on exit]

Paris! How I love being in spring sun soaked Paris. What a place it is to review and to start afresh. Amongst the many marvels of the city, how wonderful it is to wander the ways of the Seine.

Ah yes! Alongside the Seine, wandering past the tree and merchant lined paths that run from the Louvre and continue all the way to Notre Dame. How pleasant and easy it is to make ones way in the land of the Seine as it flows unconsciously past so many tributes to time and the human imagination.

Sometime not so long ago I was on such a walk when, having just passed Quai de Voltaire, and La Rue d' Awakening, I looked down a side street and noticed a museum I had not seen before. Walking towards it I noticed its name, "La Musee de Realite Sujectif, et L'Exibicion de Bouche Miniscule." [The Subjective Reality Museum and the Sleight of Mouth Exhibition]

Take a look, I thought, could be interesting. Entering through a revolving door that seemed to revolve many more times than it possibly could, or should, I was met by a tall sadly sardonic man, who spoke more like a London cab driver than a Parisian guide.

"Been 'ere before sir?"

"No." I said

"I'll be your guide then sir, if you ain't been 'ere before"

"Actually" I said tentatively, "I'd rather not have a guide, if it's all the same to you"

"Ah, well, sir, it's not all the same to me, and you not having been 'ere before like! Well, you'll need a guide. Nobody who 'ain't been 'ere before gets in without a guide, sir"

"And the cost?" I enquired politely

"There's no charge sir. It only costs you if you 'av been 'ere before!"

"Strange idea" I commented.

"Strange to those who ..."

"haven't been here before" I continued.

My guide almost smiled. It was, I reflected, more the suppressed smile of satisfaction then the smile of lighthearted humour.

"May I have a map?"

"Yes, sir. I'm not sure how useful it will be to you right now, sir, but you can have a map."

"What do you mean?"

"Map's just that, sir. The map might keep you from getting lost, or it might actually get you lost. Generally it's useful to remember that we only and always operate from a map, one map or another. But if a map is the only thing you ever look at, you won't learn a thing in this place, sir. It's the experience that counts"

"Hmmmm ... lets get started, then" I said, with a sense of what might be described as guarded enthusiasm.

Before us was a large doorway with a notice stating "Open for Reframing"

"Odd?!" I said to my guide

"Lot of people who 'aven't been 'ere before say that, sir. We do have a "Closed – without frame" section, but there's nothing in it, sir. Everything has a frame of some sort, you see, and we like to think people will enjoy changing them frequently. Not, mind you, if they haven't been 'ere before and especially if they haven't experienced reframing before!"

"What do you mean?"

"Good question, sir! Just that! When you look at any picture Sir, what it is or what it means to you, is affected by the frame you put on it. That's not to say there's a right way or a wrong way. It's more about being aware of the framing possibilities."

"The framing possibilities?"

"Yes, Sir. It's like opening your mind up Sir! Not literally though – that would be painful, and this ... well ... this, according to those I accompany, is enjoyable and some even describe it as fun, Sir."

"Ooh" I said, enthusiasm increasing.

"First, then, Sir, I think we'll look at the two large rooms – so you can get a feel for the place. These first one will help to give you a context for everything else"

"Is that because a frame is a bit like a context?"

"Yes, very good sir."

\*                    \*                    \*

The guide led me into a large rectangular room. Chandeliered, ceiling stuccoed, and frequently alcoved, the walls were filled with paintings of people. People who were being like people are and doing what people do. Sometimes, where the walls had no painting, the words "Where and When" had been painted. In the floor was inlaid the word 'Contexts'.

The first picture was of "Mr. Talk too Much"

"I don't like that. Don't like people who talk too much"

"I'm wonderin', Sir, if you could consider when or where talking too much could be useful?"

"Well, at a quiet party I suppose"

"Anywhere else?"

"When someone has to make a long presentation"

"Next picture, sir"

The next was "Mr. Rarely says anything"

"Ooh! That can be so embarrassing" I said.

"Maybe it can, sir, yet, when or where could such behaviour be appropriate or even beneficial Sir."

"Ha!, at a party where there are lots of Mr. Talk too Muches!" I quipped

"And, where or when else?"

"When someone wants quiet company, or when someone has lots of confidential information, or in a really noisy nightclub, or ..."

"You're gettin' the idea, Sir. Next"

The third was "Mrs. Definite About Everything". On seeing her I was immediately surprised when her eyes fixed on me, and then her face three dimensioned out of the picture. Her lips parted and she said...

"I'm so definite about everything that people tell me so and I feel it's such an awful thing to be. I'm definite about that too!"

"Yet" I said quickly, "where and when could being definite about everything be a really useful trait?"

"In a crisis, or when a clear decision needs to be made or when there are a lot of equivocators about." she responded – definitely.

"So you might, definitely change your definite view about how it is to be definite then?"

"Yes, definitely!" and with that she returned to two dimensions. There was now the hint of a smile on her face. The hint was enough to make me think that Mrs. Definite About Everything would be a "moaner" no longer. I thought it better not to share my internal humour with my guide.

"Time to move on, sir"

"To another useful place or time!"

"Yes, Sir. Something like that"

"I suppose everything can be useful in some context or other."

"That's a frame in itself, Sir." He said, as he led me out of the room via an exit, which was not a doorway, to another room. The exit was actually through a flap, which had been unnoticed before the guide unzipped it in a previously unblemished area of wall.

*       *       *

The triangular flap was the opening to a tent. A large tent. The contents of the tent included paintings by the score, sculptures a plenty, drawings, textiles, furniture and just about everything art-like one could imagine. Quite a lot of it, to my mind, seemed fairly abstract. Reflectively, I said to my guide ...

"What to make of all this?"

"Exactly, Sir!" he replied

I walked to an exhibit which interested me.

"Just a red square!"

"And, Sir, what might it mean?"

"It might be red squared ... and yet ... it could be ... emotion ... Strong emotion ... love or anger."

"Oh, good, Sir ... fancy noticin' how close the two can be. And?"

"It might be, panic or, the Kremlin ... or it could mean Manchester United or Arsenal or ..."

"Enough, Sir, Enough! I think you're getting the idea."

I moved on to another, which I recognized as L'Eglise D'Anvers by Van Gogh. It is the portrait of a church, with misshapen roof and walls, a "v" shaped gravel path surround along which a woman walks away. The sky and the windows of the church are a deep, deep blue, almost too deep to be true. What might it mean? I mused. I remembered seeing it in the Musee D'orsay next to a late self portrait and saw the similarity, the gravel being just like the stubble, and those sad too deep blue eyes. Yet this church was more than sad. The structure was collapsing, the blue too deep for even sadness, and the only person in the picture was walking away from the painter. Was this the last self-portrait?

"You alright, Sir?"

"Hmmm, yes, I was just wondering what it might mean"

"Everything in 'ere's a bit like that, sir. You see something and you make your mind up what it is or what it means and so often there could be another meaning. Such, sir, if you don't mind me sayin', is life!"

"You mean that when things happen, the meaning there is, is the meaning we make of it? Its like a kaleidescope of possibilities, shake it and you see a different picture"

"You're a room or two ahead of yourself, Sir."

"You mean like I'm putting the cart before the horse"

"Exactly Sir, now ..."

"You mean like a train that doesn't stop at the station it should stop at?"

"Stop it sir, not here! Metaphor room only"

"You mean I'm ahead of myself"

"Yes sir"

"And that means I'm being inappropriate, doesn't it"

"Or, that you are particularly good at persisting on a train of thought"

"Or maybe, I just can't concentrate!"

"Or maybe, you like variety"

"Or maybe I've a mind like a butterfly"

"What? Very beautiful, if somewhat metaphorical?"

"Thank you" I said. "I could stay in here forever"

"And if you do so sir, the likely consequence is that you'll be removed and taken away in a little white van! Or end up like your friend Vincent, if you catch my drift"

"Where next?" I smiled.

"Model room." replied my guide and we left the tent, content with what I had learned and moved into a fascinating place.

*       *       *

Inside there were all sorts of models and maps. There were globes of all different shapes and sizes. Some were smooth, some had terrain. There were two-dimensional maps on the walls and there were all sorts of intriguing maps lying or standing on tables. Of those on the tables, some were rectangular and flat and some were in three dimensions. I wasn't sure of the artist.

What was most amazing was the sheer variety of frames and maps. There were frames that looked like nothing I'd ever seen before, frames that must have come from some far distant, far different culture. Truly amazed, I touched a globe.

"Is the Pacific Ocean really like this?" I asked

"No sir, it's wet and 'as fish in it."

"And ..." I continued, moving to a terrained rectangular table ...

"Do the Himalayas feel like this?"

"No sir, they're colder."

"So, why do we build all these models?"

"Well, I suppose they help us navigate, sir, and actually, we can't do with out them!"

"What?"

"Yeh! It's the whole thing in a way sir. Model of the world is a sort of large frame and it's a bit like what we said earlier about maps. We always operate from our model of the world – however rich or poor that map may be."

"And there are many poor ones."

"And many rich ones too, sir"

"Depends on how you look at it"

"Exactly, Sir! Time to move on?"

"I'd like to go to the loo, please"

"That's over the road, sir"

"What, the loo?"

"Yes sir, you'll have to leave and go across the road to the other bank."

"It's in a bank – across the road?"

"No sir, its in itself ..., the Louvre"

"I'm getting confused"

"That means you are learning something sir."

"No, it means I need the toilet"

"Why didn't you say so sir? It's this way ..."

He pointed me into the strangest, oldest sort of toilet I had ever encountered. There were footprints on the floor for your feet and a hole in the floor for the obvious. Where do you sit? Where's the chain? And what! No privacy! Disgusting! These people just don't know how to build a proper toilet do they?

"Dear oh dear. That really shouldn't be allowed, should it?"

"Had enough of models of the world sir?"

"Very strange!" I replied "Not sure I got much from that"

"Just what I was thinking sir, and if you don't mind me saying so, sir, a bit like a brick wall trying to bang itself on your head without you noticing."

"What do you mean?"

"We'll see sir, we'll see."

*   *   *

We moved on. Up escalators, down steps, and through doors until we came to a door marked "The reflexive room".

"I'm still confused." I said. My guide opened the door and as I walked through I was amazed. More sculptures, drawings and pictures, yet all of me!! Embarrassed, and rarely pleased, I looked at the many representations.

"I'm really confused now" I said.

"You confuse yourself by thinking that" said the guide.

For some reason I laughed. In fact, I laughed quite a lot.
"How you cheer yourself up by doing that sir."
"Do I?"
"Oh yes, sir. Mr. Erickson, one of our original curators, used to encourage his associates to be able to laugh at themselves. He thought it very healthy."
"I think I interest myself in finding that an interesting comment."
"Excellent sir. Unlike the model room, you seem to have the essence of this room."
"Nevertheless, I think I'd like to get out of here!" I said. "Where next?" I asked
"Well, it all depends," said my guide.

*        *        *

"On What" and with that I was beckoned out of the reflexive, rather too self obsessed room, and into, well, into... a room entitled, "Very important only."
"Why are we going in here?" I asked
"Because it's important." he said, triumphantly.
"Oh, why is it important to go into the Very Important Only Room"
"Because its important to know what's important sir."
"And why is that important?" I said trumpingly.
"Well sir, when you know what is important – what's important to you – then you can choose easily or it can help you to prioritize, or even see things differently."
"I'm bothered because I still don't know the value of what's important?"
"And sir, do let me ask you, what's important about that to you?"
"It is important because I want to learn"
"Ah, so what's important to you is that you learn, sir. Being clear about that helps you to express yourself, make decisions and lets you know what troubles you on occasions."
"Ah."
"Penny dropped Sir?
"Dropped and learnt" I replied, "Nice metaphor that"
"I'm very sorry sir. That was me speaking out of room"
"And what's important about that for you?" I asked, glowing in my own cleverness
"It is important that I guide people clearly in each room so that the meaning and the importance of each room is clear sir."
"Clear, like the stars on a cloudless, moonless night, and what's important to you about guiding people clearly?"

129

"Now, now sir, clearly learning has been established, so I suggest we move on.

*           *           *

We left the room full, no doubt, of art of the highest value, and moved into, into a space. It was a circular space, a circular space with many exits. It was a white roundabout of space, where there were no doorways, simply a multitude of corridors leading off from the central space.

"I'm certainly confused by this." I said, feeling somewhat repetitious! I was still of the opinion that being confused was not a particularly desirable or pleasant sensation.

"This sir" my guide explained "is the Roundaboutcome Room"

"I'm feeling no better for having it named. Some sort of explanation might help."

"Well, sir, you know when you come to a roundabout on a road and you have many possible exits. How do you know which one to take?"

"It depends on where you want to go"

"Exactly so sir. So when you're confused or unsure, one possible way forward is to consider or reconsider the direction you want to take; to be clear about what you want and where you want to go."

"So?"

"Well, let me ask you sir. Rather that being confused, what would you prefer to be?"

"I'd like to be clear" and immediately one route leading from the round room was all blue sky, white buildings and open road. The name of the road was "Route de Clarite."

"Anything else you'd prefer, sir"

"Yes, I'd like to be cheerful" and just as the words left my mouth so another road appeared - full of smiling faces, chatting and laughing. In the distance I could hear three cheers.

"It's as if I only have to think of what I want and the road appears!"

"Precisely, sir, and if I may say so sir, such is the 'uman condition. Sadly few are aware of it. As a result, if you don't consider what you want it is so easy to just go round and round."

"Like the Circle Line." I interjected.

"What?"

"Oh, it's something we have in London. A railway line that just goes round and round."

"So that means you can only visit where you've been before?"

"Hmmm. Yes."

"We don't have anything like that on the Metro sir. 'Ere everythin' is defined by the destination!"

"We do have some like that. However, even when we do, and especially on the District Line there can be so many different destinations that you have to check constantly to make sure you're going in the right direction."

"If I may say so sir, all that constant conscious checking doesn't do anybody any good. It simply serves to add doubt and concern to the goal."

"So, if I'd like to have wealth, a house, a better job." As I spoke, so roads sprang out of the roundabout, each with an appropriate representation.

"So, where shall we go, sir?"

"At the moment, how about New Learning" And as I said it a most unusual road appeared. It was a road with many twists and turns, with many suspended pennies, and with many trick walls at odd angles. I almost said what I was feeling to my guide, but one look and one moments reflection encouraged me to choose to say,

"Some people might consider this a confusing road"

"Well done, sir. The road to learning is a very splendid thing! Or should I say, a many pennied thing." The chuckle suggested he was obviously making some kind of joke.

As we walked down the twists and turns, I added

"It just depends on your model of the world, doesn't it." As I said this one of the trick walls clouted me forcefully on the head, and the air was suddenly filled with the clatter of pennies dropping, as if from heaven!

"No, don't go there sir, not yet anyway" said my guide apparently capable of mind reading!

"Why not?"

"Different building sir, and no apparent exit! Personally, the idea of perpetual joy seems a bit lacking in variety, but my own guide is considering me for a bit of personal development. She thinks I'm on the brink of requiring something spiritual. Tells me it'll make all the difference! Anyway, that's enough of me sir. Let's have a look over here...."

*            *            *

And just around a many pennied, red walled corner, I could make out a distant gallery, or was it close, or was it ...

Instantly a door frame was before me. Above the door was a circular face with twelve large freckles and a twitching moustache. The door itself was wood framed with long rectangular glass and in the glass swung a pendulum. An inscription read, " Le grand père de temps" [The grandfather of time.]

"Shall we go in?" I asked..

"No time like the present, sir"

I pushed and the door swung open and I walked into a narrow corridor, like an arete slope, with huge space on either side. There was sand all over the place, sand that was shifting this way and that, running here and there and everywhere. And there were clocks. Clocks of all sizes and shapes, some going forwards, some going backwards, some "Dali-esque" and many crumbling into sand, which is how everything seemed to end.

"What now?" I said

"Exactly sir!" my less than helpful guide responded. More helpfully, he continued...

"You see sir, there is only now. The past is a figment of the memory and the future a figment of the imagination."

"Oh!"

"And if whatever you are thinking is in any way troublesome, you could probably put that thought into the past and simply focus on what is real and present now and even have a positive aspiration for the future!"

"That isn't helpful" I replied

"No sir. It wasn't helpful a few moments ago, and if you simply make yourself aware of your present capabilities and possibilities, then it might just be helpful in the future."

"I'm feeling stupid"

"No sir, you were feeling stupid yet if you trust yourself to learn, then in a minute or two you'll possibly feel clever."

"So if I understand this, you can simply put negative things behind you, be positive about your self and see positive thing in the future?"

"Yes sir, that's about the size of it."

"Gosh, I'm feeling really quite clever."

As I spoke these words, a sign appeared on one side of the corridor. On it were written the words,

"As you liked it."

On the other side of the corridor,

"What you will"

The sands of time stopped for just a moment. All in the corridor was absolutely still, seemingly balanced, and quietly peaceful.

"Now." I said, unsure whether the word was a question or a statement. I'm not sure how long the moment lasted.

"Lets move on", he said.

A spell was broken.

"What was all that about?"

"You almost went somewhere else sir"

"Was it alright?"

"If it was good for you sir! You do know you can go there anytime, anywhere, don't you sir?"

"I think I do."

"Then that's a little bonus sir. Ah, the lift."

*          *          *

We walked into the museum lift and after several moments in which there was no sensation of going up, down or sideways, we walked out of the other side, into a gallery full of oriental paintings.

"Where am I?" I asked.

"The Gallery of Chun King" my guide replied. "Very significant artist but not as well known as he might be, on account of people keeping his art to themselves and others not even knowing they've got it."

"Oh." I said

The first room was entitled "simple Chun King". Here, everything was arranged in fives. A central picture had one further picture above, one below and one on either side. The central picture was of a small bird resting on a twig in a blossoming cherry tree. Below it was just the bird in what seemed like larger focus, and above it was the whole tree with the bird in it. To one side was a different kind of bird and on the other different types of twig.

"Just a matter of shifting perspectives in a particular way and of seeing things at different levels.

"Basically yes, sir. It is, however, a bit more than that. With nearly every, or any, thing, you can go up down or sideways as you think about it!"

"Oh."

"Doin'this can encourage flexibility, maybe creativity, and often fun."

"And Chun King?"

"What you've just looked at was part of the early experiments sir, after which a whole movement has followed called the Chunking movement or experience."

"And what do the Chunking movement do?"

"Well sir, you'll be sorry to hear this, but they go ..."

"Up, down or sideways" I said

"Take this chair, sir"

"Where to?"

"Now, now sir. Chunk down"

"Er ... the seat"

133

"Chunk up, sir"

"Er ... Furniture?"

"Good sir, yet, its like levels of a taxonomy"

"You can't (a) fool (a) me" I replied. "There ain't no tax on (a) me" and laughed. My guide looked to me, and through me, seemingly unaware of my allusion.

"Do you like films?" I asked.

"Not a lot sir."

"And, more specifically, have you ever heard of the Marx Brothers?"

"No sir, but if you were to take different Engels on it, I might." he said, looking at me sideways! There might have been a smile on his face, but I wasn't certain. He continued, "Anyway, let's not harp on about that one now, and if it's not too cheeky of me, I'll suggest we zip off back to the topic of the chair sir, before we get at all grouchy. What about sideways?"

"Er ... stool ... or bed ... Or table ..."

"Excellent sir, now for the second room."

We walked into the strangest place. We were walking on thick, strong glass. Above us and below were more or less equal conical shapes one opening up, the other becoming more and more narrow. Above, the shape went on higher than you could see, and below us the conical narrowing went further than you could look.

"Chun King's latter work" my guide confirmed, "was about continual up and down chunking, which he began to believe lead almost inevitably to the same place.

"What?"

"Well, if you go down and down for anything you get to something you can't actually see so you build a theory about it and then collect some evidence. If you go up and up you similarly get to a place where beliefs and assumptions take over and the same thing happens. We build a theory."

So I looked up as far as I could, to beyond where things were depicted. As the view went beyond my sight there was simply some light. As I looked down, then, beyond the realm of identifiable things was the same sense of light.

"Time, so to speak, to move on sir. Don't want to do a Chun King sir!"

"What's that?"

"Well sir, after this second experiment, Chun stopped painting and went to his 'Severely Profound Place', where he thought a lot and produced nothing."

"Was he alright?"

"Reports are, sir, that he was extremely happy."

"He'd obviously got a good pension."

If my guide had ever given me a strange, disconcerting look, it was at that moment.

Anyway, eventually we moved on, and whether we went through a door, a window or even a looking glass, I don't truly remember.

*    *    *

We were now surrounded by a plethora of fully stocked bars, shop counters, and tills. At one end of this long hall of a room there was an unusual throne. I had never seen one so exceptional.

As I walked up to the first bar, my guide manifested himself behind it.

"Yes Sir?"

"Oh, I never know what to order?"

"Tell me sir," he began "has there not been one occasion on which you knew what to order?"

"Well" I began "yes, there was the time when Jules told me to get myself a beer. I only know what to do when someone else tells me."

"Tell me sir," he said, sounding suspiciously and annoyingly clever, "excusing my present presence, has there not been one occasion on which you have made your own mind up without someone else being there? – like coming into this gallery?" He smiled, annoyingly!

"OK, but you'll not catch me again"

"Sir ..." The look of pleasure on his face was the most maddening I had yet to experience. "Has there not been one occasion on which you believed that you'd not be caught again and you were, ha, ha!" It was not so much a laugh as an incitement to violence!

"I've never been so annoyed in my life!"

"Tell me sir, do you remember that time when ..."

I picked up the nearest object and threw it at him. The large chocolate egg went straight through him.

"You're not real," I said.

"Lot of people say that, sir" he retorted

"Are you one of these people who've been on one of those courses?"

"No sir, I just work here!"

"What is this place?"

"This, sir, is the counter example room."

"And what's the throne?"

"That throne sir, is for an exceptional ruler, but we can't find one."

"Excuse me," I exclaimed in the throws of pleasure. "There's always an exceptional rule ... er ... somewhere."

"Exactly sir, Well done! Lesson complete."

I don't know whether I became madder or not, but I heard the sound of pennies

dropping in a corridor nearby.

"Can we go somewhere else, please?"

"Of course, sir."

"Is there a metaphor room?"

"Yes, sir."

"Can we go there?"

"Don't think we need to sir."

"But, I want to."

"I know sir, but you'll be disappointed."

"No I won't."

"Maybe later, but for now, it's time we went in to a rather special room."

*         *         *

And he opened another hitherto invisible zipped flap, which led into a massive tent with the most horrible pictures in it. Murders, cruelty, everyday rudeness, they were all there, all in their glorious gore.

"This is horrid." I exclaimed.

"They've all got positive intent, sir!"

"What! What about that?" I protested as I saw a portrayal of a person kicking a cat.

"Just passing on anger, sir!"

"So, how's that positive?"

"Well, sir, it's positive for the person who is expressing, or getting rid of, or passing on the anger. I'm not saying it's positive for the cat, or the onlooker."

"So, what about bombers?"

"Hmmm, whoever it is usually believes they are doing the "right" thing for a "good" purpose. Sometimes, intent is difficult to see sir, especially from one's own perspective, yet if one presumes positive intent is there then it makes understanding easier. Now, for an artist or a performer, it is relatively easy to spot intent."

"The intent of the artist?"

"Yes, sir, you can always fall back on the wish to stimulate, educate or to awaken."

"Ah, yes, I suppose you could put everything in the positive intent category, but there again, there'd be an exception, and it would almost certainly depend on your model of the world, wouldn't it?"

"Sir, you are making my day. We're nearly there!"

"Where?"

"Where? To the summation of your journey, sir. We are nearly at what one

might call "the end", but that in itself is a mere temporal irrelevance and, of course, is a figment of the imagination in itself."

"What?"

"Nearly finished, sir, is what I should have said."

"So can I visit the metaphor room? Please?"

"You'll be disappointed, sir."

"No. Promise I won't."

"Alright then sir."

*        *        *

For the first time my guide seemed unsure of himself. He began to walk like a tentative deer, ever alert for a sign of danger. We walked through what seemed like a dense forest of bamboo, it was dark, enclosed, wood tight of space, yet in a way it was more like walking in a swimming pool, with water up to your waist, yet in a way it was more like meandering across endless sand dunes, yet.... it was none of these. It was only like them, and in being like them, so different images and perceptions of what this space might be like abounded in the possible consciousness and new and different meanings were being made.

At the end of whatever it was, was a doorway unlike any other doorway, which led into a room unlike any other room.

"It's impossible to describe this." I said

"What are you like, sir?"

"I mean, an entrance without a doorway, a room without walls. The possibilities for description are endless."

"Quite so sir."

I was, however, not to be disappointed for in the centre of whatever it was that I couldn't describe was a vast yet visible representation of Paris. Paris by late evening bright light. Paris, springtime full of flowers and cherry blossom. Paris full of people, Paris full of life.

My eye was led to the Seine, and as I looked along its banks I was drawn to a brightly lit museum. The museum, I could see, had many splendid rooms and much splendid architecture. There were marvelous paintings and sculptures too, and only two people inside. It took a moment or two. They were moments I'll remember forever.

Standing clearly in the most indescribably wondrous room which seemed to change in its very essence in each moment, were two men. One was my guide and the other looked very much like me. They were looking at a representation of Paris.

"What does this all mean?" many of me asked many guides. I looked up through

a window and saw a large face beginning to laugh. I was beginning to laugh. The sound of joyous laughter filled my ears, as I began to laugh loudly.

Astonished, I turned and felt myself in a revolving door once more. Suddenly, I was alone. I was standing alone and I was once again by the Seine.

I was back in the land of the Seine, or rather, by the Seine. I considered that the Seine was never going to be quite the same again.

Since that time I have scoured the Rues of the area but inevitably I find myself on the Boulevard Saint Michel or some other place. I've never been able to find that gallery again. On one of my searches, however, I did see a sign, which read:
Les Routes de Perseé, "Once opened, we can never be closed."

I have written this record so that you too may share the experience, just in case you do not find the Musee in your own Seine walks.

**La Musee [Reframing Map]**

After the introductory journey, through the door:

Simple Reframing:
Context
Content

Some Sleight of Mouth like patterns:
Model of the World
Refer to Self
Values
Outcomes
Time
Chunking
Counter Example
Positive Intention
Metaphor

# Part Four

# Metaphor

# 23

# The "Tensed Spool"

When a person wants to learn something and wants to learn it well, it is often a good idea to ask an expert. It is even better if the learner has a strong sense of curiosity and a bundle of enthusiasm. Encompassed with these senses and with a thirst for learning, the youthful yet not necessarily young woman went to see the man who knew something about metaphor. Metaphor was the present object of her enthusiasm and curiosity.

The man she went to see was, of course, dressed most strangely, but not with a pointed hat or star covered cloak. Rather, his large brown boots seemed slightly too big for his frame and his trousers showed signs of having tramped along a muddy path. He was not particularly tall, yet his large face seemed to beam towards her from above. His searching gaze encouraged her to become slightly too aware of her waif-like frame and her tangled long hair. This increased her tendency to look away from the gaze of his eyes.

"Tell me about metaphor, if you please. What is metaphor for and how would you construct one?" she enquired, with the congruence of innocence.

"There are many reasons for metaphor." He began. "Probably the most important is that metaphor encourages a recipient to search deeply for meaning, to search deeply for meaning inside. It is there, after all, where the answers lie, the answers that will make most sense. And metaphor allows you to say things that you might not say directly."

He paused for just a few moments and then began to smile. It was the kind of smile that comes from inside, the smile of impending pleasure.

"If I am to tell you of metaphor, then I might well begin with a story.

The story is of a young boy who loved films, who loved the cinema and the tales told therein. He loved the cinema so much and he wanted to see as many films

as he could. So, he decided to help the old man who worked in the projection booth. From there he could watch many films and watch them over and over. So, he helped to unload the spools from their cases, and mount them precisely on the projector. And then on occasions he set them to run. How he grew to love that sound. Switch, click, r,r,r,r,roll.

The young boy found something of interest in every film and he took great pleasure in learning. Whilst he learnt about stories and learnt about films he was also determined to become a projectionist, one as excellent as the old man.

He would watch the old man again and again and in doing so, he would notice. He would notice how the old man moved his hands, and how and where he looked. Then he would notice the care and the checks that preceded every move. In his mind he would then imagine himself doing each of these skilful, deft movements. He remembered sequences that the old man used and carefully repeated. Occasionally he'd ask a question in order to check understanding.

"To be a projectionist, one like you, what is of greatest importance?"

The old man answered in a strange way,

"I don't actually think of myself as a projectionist. That is simply what I do. It is more important to consider my purpose, my function in playing these films. I prefer to see myself as one who helps provide pleasure, as one who encourages others to experience in new and different ways, and as one who might even encourage people toward undiscovered territories."

"And enterprises of great pith and moment?" added the boy.

"What?"

"Nothing!" Said the boy.

"And at a more practical level" the old man continued, "it is of greatest importance to ensure that you have a tensed spool."

"A tensed spool?" asked the boy.

"Yes, that's so important, and you know," the old man went on, "I'm reminded of a story.

This is a story of a youthful woman with straight hair and a tousled disposition. She had embarked upon a journey, as we all eventually do. At first she believed herself to be on a journey to somewhere, to a place that is, in fact, to Budapest. Fairly soon, she began to realise that the "somewhere" was incidental. Rather, she knew herself to be on that journey we all engage in, at some time or other in life.

Even so, to be in that city was an absolute delight and she was encouraged to learn, to learn more about that place. She found out that what she had thought of as one had once upon a time been two. Originally there were two towns, one

called Buda and the other called Peste. The two were close yet so divided. One was high above the Danube and housed the glorious castle. This side of the river was Buda. The other side was low and flat and was the seat of the Parliament. This side of the river was Peste. Funny, she thought. Funny that government was on the low side. She explored each of the towns, both Peste and the other side, the higher side, called Buda.

Whilst on her journey, she met a man, someone very special. To be with this person lifted her spirit, left her feeling enriched. It was as if she could see all before her, and quieten her inner voice. Her inner voice of disdain and disquiet that often had troubled her mind. She felt herself, at last, to truly be at peace.

On their walks around the city, the place they liked to visit was the cafe on the high side, close to the fisherman's basilica. There they would sit for hours and whilst they talked she would love to look, to look through the arched glassless windows at the winding river below. And on the other side of the Danube, she looked at the Parliament. How small it seemed from this place on high, so small and easily managed.

One time she asked him, quietly and firmly, with interest more than a need to know, because in a way she knew.
"Who are you really and what might I call you?"

He looked at her, and whilst she began to consider those names by which she might possibly call him, he replied to her and said,

"I'd like to tell you a story. A story of several sticks of celery determined to embark upon an adventure, a very special adventure. The adventure they chose, maybe because it had become so popular in recent years, was to climb Mount Everest. Not knowing each other awfully well, when they met and assembled at base camp, they encouraged themselves to interact and exercise together so that they might become something of a bunch. Once they had indeed begun to bond, they began their adventure, their journey of achievement. As they clambered over the early slopes, so they gained in confidence and mutual respect. The plateau and peaks that they crossed and climbed exacted their collective sinews yet enabled them to grow stronger in the enjoyment of their company and in an ever increasing sense of meaning and purpose. Then one particular day, after crossing a crevasse and struggling through snow, they came to a sheer precipitous cliff. Snow, ice and bare rock overhung their upward staring eyes and much of the celery blanched at the prospect of what might be one cliff climb too far. They looked at each other, eyes on stalks, and pondered how they could carry on and overcome this obstacle on their epic journey. It was in such thought that they stood, looking up and searching their striated surfaces for a solution. As they stood there, some of them began to complain,

145

"We can't do this."
"It's too difficult"
"We're not capable of such a feat."
Then one of their more reflective members spoke, so that all could hear,

"I am reminded of a story. It is a tale told of the second best therapist in history, the celebrated Hugh Kanduit.
Hugh was in his room one day, when he heard a patient knock at the door,
"Come in" Hugh Kanduit said and as he said this, the man walked in. Hugh asked him,
"Who are you?"
"Ian Martin Hapless. I.M.Hapless."
"How are you?" asked Hugh.
"I am hapless."
"And what is your problem?" asked Hugh, even though he predicted the answer.
"I am hapless" continued the man.
"How would you prefer to be?" enquired Hugh Kanduit and as Ian Martin was pondering a reply Hugh made an interjection. This was highly unusual for Hugh as he was a well trained coach and a counsellor of the Rogerian mode to boot.
He did, however, know the value of choice and flexibility of approach.
"You know, Ian Martin, you remind me of someone who came to see me some time ago. I will tell you his story.

His name was Uriah, Uriah Sucksess, who believed himself a failure. That always makes me laugh, said Hugh, because I know it is not true. It's not true of him, it's not true of you. So this is what I said,
You only need to make one small change, and that change is very simple. You need to change your name to Uara, rather than be a Uriah. Put simply, Uara Sucksess and then you'll find that all will be well. You might think of this change as profound, or not. All I would say is that it's a choice, and certainly you can do it."

After a pause, Hugh then asked,
"What is the small change that you can make, patient Ian Martin?"
And after another not too long pause, he further said,
"You can do it too, can't you?"
Ian Martin replied,
"I am happy with that. Is that right?"
"That's right, that's very right."

Hugh Kanduit bade Ian farewell and as the patient walked to the door, Hugh Kanduit called out,
"Remember Sucksess, Remember Uara, Remember Uara Sucksess". Ian nodded as Hugh knew he would do, as Ian was externally referenced. Hugh had not bothered to tell Ian Martin, now happy, about Uara marrying Bea, as he thought Ian Martin was happy enough. Happy, for now at least.

So, the reflective celery said,
"You know what Hugh Kanduit would say to us as we all stand here now. He would say, "Believe you can do it", and he would tell us to band together and in that bunch to use our skills and then he would he would add to us all,
"You can do whatever you want and achieve whatever you put your mind to. You simply have to trust and believe that you can do it."
    And so they did. They bound themselves together and using all their present skill, they stalked their way up the awesome cliff until they reached a plateau. On this plateau they moved on once again, adding more strength and perception. Adding new bits of growth as they strode, new bits of skill and experience.
[Whether you know this now or not, do you know what happens when you add a bit to celery? Well, you get a celebrity! That's right.]
    That is what happened as they journeyed on. They became exactly the sort of celery that they wanted to be. Celery you could truly celebrate being. They would ponder upon the first of their kind that ever achieved this feat, Edmund it was, and as they continued their journey, they felt more and more relaxed, no tensing at all! Each new peak was seen as a challenge, as achievement that would undoubtedly aid and add to their personal greenery.

And whilst they looked down from Buda, she continued and made some suggestions, "Guide, or teacher, holy or wise one, companion or special soul."
"I notice," he replied, "that all the indexes that you suggest are rather reverential. So I suggest that you shift the index and call me simply "friend". I am undoubtedly sometimes one thing and on occasions, another. So, whenever you tell a story, change the referential index, change it frequently."
    The woman, now with tousled hair and a lovely disposition, smiled and knew without contradiction, that you can be all of these. Peste, from across the Danube, seemed so far below, yet she knew it was a part of the city, as vital as the Buda. Recognising those two diverse parts was the key to moving forward. They worked together so well, she and her guide and friend.

"Yes," said the old man, "a tensed spool is important because it is always the story

in the story, the journey in the journey, the play within the play, that's where we catch the conscious conscience of the king."

"So you do know your Shakespeare, don't you?" said the wise young man. "Might I suggest "nested loops" as opposed to a tensed spool?"

"What a very good idea" said the old projectionist, still keen to learn. "Even a tensed spool can use a little transformation. And the elements are more or less the same. I agree, nested loops."

And the man who knew of metaphor continued and said that another way to use the skill was to do with embedding commands and influencing the mind of the listener to encourage new connections.

"Oh," enquired the woman, "How?"

His eyes lit up once more,

"Wouldn't it be nice if every time you saw a piece of celery you remembered Hugh Kanduit, and Uara Sucksess, and I M Happy?

Wouldn't it be interesting if every time you had a mountain to climb you would remember Hugh Kanduit.

The least all that would do is to make you chuckle rather than all that tensing.

And wouldn't it be wonderful if whenever and wherever you ever went, you remembered Budapest, knowing that for every pest in your life there is the other side, that higher side called Buda. And then you'd probably realise that you need to have both in your life. They're both required for growth. C'est la vie!"

"Did you say celery?" she asked.

"You can have too much of a good thing", he replied and added,

"Never explain a metaphor. If you do you might stop the searching for new and further meaning."

"And are there any other reasons for metaphors?"

"They certainly can be fun."

She left happy and relaxed, thinking of Hilary, or was it ...?

# 24

# Tellers of Tales

Sitting. Sitting in the top floor teashop of a local department store reading the chocolate runes atop my cappuccino. Sitting and waiting. Waiting for Christine, reflecting that I might prefer to meet her some other time, when I would be less preoccupied.

The preoccupation was preparing my weekend training. The weekend was supposed to be covering metaprograms and metaphors. The metaprogram part was fairly clear in my head. However, I was still uncertain as to how I might weave together the metaphorical concepts I had chosen to put before the would-be master practitioners and my mind continued to search as I scoured the runes. The two main concepts were "The Hero's Journey", and the idea of life scripts. Poetry was certainly going to be part of the connecting fabric, and my mind was zig-zagging between the search for stories that would waft and weft their way through the day, and reciting Robert Frost's "Stopping by Woods on a Snowy Evening" and "The Road not Taken".

The notion of "The Hero's Journey" was a la Robert Dilts, Steven Gilligan and Joseph Campbell, and is that our lives and life challenges, are akin to the journeys of mythic heroes in classical literature.

The concept concerning the significance of scripts and stories suggests that we live our lives according to the stories we listened to and loved in our childhood. Key to the session would be two sequential questions. The first, "Tell the story of your favourite fairy tale from childhood in about two minutes", followed up by the show-stopping question, "And how is that the story of your life so far?"

As Christine walked in, something was different. She seemed taller, more assured and moved in a relaxed, flowing and easy way. She offered to get me some food, but I was in no mood for eating.

"Hello. How are yoooo?" We chorused.

"We're just about to move back in to our house." She said. "The rebuild is fantastic. It looks magnificent. It's almost too good to be true. You must come and see it sometime."

"You look really well." I said, my interest being more in her state than her house.

"That's funny you should say so."

"Oh?"


To my amazement she began to tell me a story. For thirty-five years she had lived under the shadow of fraternal rejection. This drama was now played out in her brother's occasional visits, which occurred when his ambassadorial role, or a family event, brought him to this country. Sometimes he arrived alone, on other occasions he would bring his family. Christine, her husband and her children had never been invited to any of the palatial dwellings he frequently occupied.

Whenever he visited, he acted as if the most necessary and urgent matter on his mind was leaving. The general coldness of his behaviour, particularly toward Christine, left her desperately uncomfortable and led her to days of destructive internal anguish.

His infrequent visits had been easy to forget once the activity of family life kicked in with sufficient intensity to break the spell.

This summer, however, was different. Her brother had visited three times in quick succession. There was no respite. There was no adequate distraction.

"And I found the key" she said, inspiring me to a series of internal reflections.

"The key" I reflected was possibly an "operating metaphor". Christine was suggesting that maybe she sees life as a series of doors, locks or boxes or that require keys. The result of finding the key was to "open" and reap rewards. Very Merchant of Venice, I thought. Then I began to consider what sorts of keys the keys may be. Jewel encrusted and gilded, black wrought iron, or miniature in silver. The possibilities were endless. I felt a "Clean Language/Grovian Metaphor" seminar coming on and resisted that temptation, maybe to our mutual loss. Like the suggestion in Frost's poem, I would keep that thought for another day, knowing I might never come back to it.

There was, however, one temptation too strong to resist. Fuelled by my own quest for weekend fabric and a little excitement, I asked,

"And what is your favourite fairy tale?"

Christine stopped, slightly taken aback.

"There are so many."

I maintained the necessary silence.

After a moment or two of thought, she began, "It's like King Lear. It is the story of a powerful king. A king who asks his children to tell him what he is to them. One by one the children tell him of his greatness and of their love and admiration, until it comes to the turn of the youngest daughter.

"You," she says to him, "are the salt in my life."

"Salt!" he shouts, enraged.

The king's banishes this youngest daughter from his presence and from his kingdom. Outcast and unsupported, like any child who loses a parent, she can only blame herself for this misery. Such a deed required atonement in the form of self inflicted punishment. She beats herself and then, in order to experience further suffering, wraps herself in stinging nettles. Even after this, she continues to mark her shame by wearing hooded garments to keep her from the gaze of the world. In the pit of her night, she resolves, eventually, to tread the harder path and return to the world. As her way back into the world of people, she takes to the life of a serving girl. As luck and her natural talent as a chef would have it, she eventually gains work as a cook, and then as a cook in a lovely palace. The palace lay in a kingdom, which was not too far and not too close to her own. Local royalty often used the palace to entertain foreign dignitaries.

And so, as you might expect, the inevitable happens. The king, her father visits the palace. The still hooded and outcast daughter begs to prepare his soup. The soup arrives, prepared by the exiled princess. She has taken care to prepare his soup without any salt.

Upon supping, the King cries out,

"Who prepared this soup?"

"I did." says a hooded figure standing in nearby shadow.

"There is no salt in this soup. I cannot abide it."

"You would like salt in your soup?" she asks.

"I must have salt in my soup. Without salt it is tasteless and bland. I cannot enjoy soup without salt." he replies.

"And I want for the salt of my life," she says and reveals herself to him.

Time stops. He stands before her utterly astonished in a charm of momentary eternity. He understands her meaning for the first time and embraces that which he had lost."

Well, there's a story, I reflected! That does for the life script! Not to be too distracted by the excitement of finding my own key, I continued my enquiry.

"Oh!" I exclaimed, "And what happened with your brother?"

Christine explained that she could contain herself no longer. She had read somewhere that only if we deal with what concerns us, does it no longer control our life.

She resolved to tell him of her feelings and her perceptions and she further decided to do this in writing. She was, after all, an English teacher and where words might fail her in interaction, her talent for expression in the written word would allow her to marshal her thoughts and express herself clearly. She wrote page upon page and then distilled the tome. When the two resultant pages were ready she recognised the real challenge. She now had to find sufficient courage to send the two pages. In those two pages, as well as expressing her feeling, she offered the sword of eternal separation. If his behaviour did mirror his intention, then to never see him again would be an appropriate solution. She steeled herself and sent the letter.

Her trial, of course, had only just begun. Now, she had to wait, and in waiting she confronted the greatest demon of them all. The one created inside the mind, by the mind, and then played out in the body. She descended into a darkness of her own making. Each night she slept not, each night was spent in worry, each night she sweated tears. As she waited for the response, her body began to close down. Stooping, aching and stiff, she could barely walk. Her voice became the outward strangled expression of her internal torture. The coldness of her brother might even be more welcoming than this desolate, desperate waiting. A deep pool was engulfing her. Above the pool, a drawn sword hung in the air, ready to perform it's final act.

(No problem with an example of the hero's journey either, I thought.)

The reply was a complete surprise. There was no acceptance of her offer. On the contrary, he stated that the cold, dismissive way she viewed his behaviour was neither a reflection of what he wished or meant.

I reflected upon a pair of subtle Presuppositions:
the most important information about a person is their
behaviour, and a person is not their behaviour.

Her life is now changing rather dramatically. Like the way a final fine grain of sand balances the scales, her body became restored, renewed and strengthened. More than that, her youngest son, who had been so difficult, began behaving in a changed, respectful manner. Nothing has been said or stated between them, there had simply been a sea change. Something rich and strange indeed. A new sense of self was now permeating every cell of her being

We then chatted briefly about all else in our respective worlds. I could have stayed there all day, yet was haunted by Frost once more, reflecting that I had a long way to go before I might rest peacefully.

Before we parted, I shared how she had given me all I needed for my weekend. I asked her if I might tell her story to my participants. I now found

my earlier thoughts about having better things to do than meet with Christine a little ironic.

Maybe it is always thus. Maybe the world presents us with all we need to notice and know just at the right time. Where there is no awareness there will be no noticing and if we are not ready to perceive, we will not see. As for me, maybe I was learning that looking interminably inside my own head for answers is probably less useful than spending time with a much-loved friend. Lucky are those of us who have such resources.

Driving back to my more native teashop, I was listening to Charles Faulkner on tape. He quotes from Sartre,
"A man is always a teller of tales. He lives surrounded by his stories and the stories of others. He sees everything that happens to him through them, and he tries to live his life as if he was telling a story."

Women do it as well, John Paul, I heard myself saying. In fact, they can do it exceedingly well.

Sitting once more. Sitting in the teashop, writing this story, and noticing with a sigh, how a conversation with Christine had made all the difference.

Part Five

# Origins and Other Thoughts

# 25

# Naven - A Personal History of NLP

Michael was presenting. All of a sudden I was transported back, back down the vista of years, and back to the time of the three-day week. Remember that? I was sitting in the reading room of my university on a night when we could have light. And I was chuckling.

I was not a particularly good student. My intellect and reasonably capable mind were sadly not matched with the ability to read vast volumes or the discipline to produce regular essays. Either of these attributes would have resulted in a better degree and in improved preparation for the rest of my life.

My chuckles concerned a book called "Naven". It had been suggested as part of my anthropology course, engagingly fronted by Mr. MacDonald. He required us to undertake a ten thousand word thesis. For mine, I had originally chosen the adolescently attractive topics of jokes and obscenity. Soon the "jokes" became discarded on the basis of a Freudian text that was not particularly funny and intellectually rather stretching.

By contrast, "Naven" met all my criteria. The chapter describing the ritual ceremonies was wonderfully amusing and gave me with the opportunity to astound my friends with descriptions of anarchic ritual behaviour, "transvesticism", and explicit sexual reference. I am sure my amusement was not the intention of the anthropologist. It was, I believe, a reflection of my questionable maturity.

One principle of the course encouraged us to see each act and behaviour as a statement of the whole culture. This would be particularly evident in ritual ceremonies, where any action was likely to demonstrate the values of the culture, the cultural beliefs about the world, the social order, the relationship between the sexes and particularly significant family relationships.

So, when in 1996 as I sat in Regent's College, London, listening to the marvellously entertaining Michael Neill as he described Robert Dilt's

Neurological levels, I had the sensation of returning to my intellectual homeland. I was overjoyed to recognise something from so many years ago.

For me to explain the Neurological levels to you now, I might do so by using the following illustration:

As you read this now you are undoubtedly doing so in an **environment** and you are undoubtedly **behaving**. Notice that the behaviour [reading] is an application of your **skills and capabilities**. Using these skills and capabilities as you carry out the behaviour in your present environment, reflects your **values** [the importance or usefulness of reading, or the importance of learning NLP, for example] and your **beliefs**. [What reading this book will enable you to do, or why it is good to read, or read about NLP in particular]. What **identity**, or special aspect of you is the you that is engaged in reading this right now? [Robert Dilts would encourage you to consider the metaphorical person or creature that would symbolise you - the reader.] Finally, what is the greater **purpose or mission** you are involved in right now? [Are you reading this in order to be able to help others, or as part of your journey to make a difference in the world, for example? Or is this the path through which you will realise even more of your own potential?]

There you have it! The six neurological levels, created by Robert Dilts*. [Values and Beliefs are considered as one level] In a way it is straightforward to believe that in anything and everything we do we express so much of ourselves. I remember being encouraged to use such an assumption when I learnt to be an interviewer in the 1970s.

So, in that moment of 1996, I resolved to find a copy of "Naven". Exeter University library no longer had the copy I had used. The original was published in 1936. Where would I find a copy? I considered spending the rest of my life travelling to the Hays, Rosses and Winchcombes of the world in permanent pursuit of the text I had treasured so long ago. A few weeks passed and I decided on the rather novel idea of asking a bookshop if they could order one! My luck was in. There had been a second edition in 1958 which had been reprinted. The tributes I read on receiving my new copy clearly demonstrated the reason for the reprint.
"The author has constructed one of the most influential works of field anthropology ever written."

"it is an elegant and revealing example of modern anthropology."
"this book ... is a classic of modern anthropological literature."

Excitedly, I reread the first chapter which described the "naven". The "naven" are ceremonies performed to celebrate notable accomplishments of young tribesmen. There is a marvellous passage where "Wau" [uncle] participates in the celebration of achievement of "Laua" [nephew]. Dressed as a female, Wau searches for Laua and on finding him,

"... he will further demean himself by rubbing the cleft of his buttocks down the length of his laua's leg, a sort of sexual salute which is said to have the effect of causing the laua to make haste to get valuables which he may present to his wau to "make him all right" ...

The wau's gesture is called mogul nggelak-ka. In this phrase the word mogul means "anus", while nggelak-ka is a transitive verb which means "grooving", e.g. ian nggelak-ka means to dig a ditch. The suffix -ka is closely analagous to the English suffix, -ing, used to form present participles and verbal nouns.
This gesture of wau I have seen only once."

So much NLP in this short passage! Linguistics was at the core of the commentary and the detached nature of the observations reflected the meta or third position. No wonder in NLP it is sometimes referred to as the anthropologist's position! This anthropological detachment is even more evident in the following example from the back of the book, where there are several pictures. The note under one photograph is as follows:
"an initiator expressing scorn for a novice by rubbing his buttocks on the latter's head. This gesture is presumably quite distinct from the gesture of the wau, who shames himself by rubbing his buttocks on his laua's leg. {**The dog in this picture belonged to the ethnographer and was not native**}"

I began to wonder just how much NLP there might be in this book. I dipped in here and there. The preface to the 1936 edition is written from St. John's College, Cambridge and the author thanks Malinowski, Radcliffe-Brown, and, not surprisingly, Margaret Mead**. In the "Epilogue" from 1936 the author writes,
"To have put forward, unsupported by a solid backing of fact, theories and hypotheses which were new, would have been criminal, but it so happens that none of my theories is in any sense new or strange. They are all to some extent platitudes, which novelists, philosophers, religious leaders, lawyers, the man in the street and even anthropologists, have reiterated in various forms probably since language was invented."

Was this the original key to modelling? Is this the answer to the sceptic? Is this the basis for the study of human excellence? Is this in some way an explanation for the apparent lack of theoretical structure and the seeming disinterest in creating NLP as an academic discipline?

In the 1958 edition, there is a new epilogue in which I found the

following passage:
"... the way is open for growth of an entirely new science-which has in fact become basic to modern thought. This new science has as yet no satisfactory name. A part of it is included within what is now called communications theory, a part of it is in cybernetics, and a part in mathematical logic. The whole is still unnamed and imperfectly envisioned."

Was this imperfect vision with no name of 1958 the driving force behind NLP? Eventually I found my way to the preface of the second edition. There
I read:
"We now have the beginnings of a general theory ...; and, in terms of the general theory, we have to re-examine all that we thought we knew about organisms, societies, families, personal relationships, ecological systems, servo-mechanisms, and the like."

Naven was written by the anthropologist, Gregory Bateson***. The second edition preface of 1958 is from Palo Alto, California.

*       *       *

Footnote* - Robert Dilts does attribute his neurological levels to Bateson, yet attributes it specifically to Bateson's levels of learning.

Footnote** - Margaret Mead, the world renowned anthropologist, was the first wife of Gregory Bateson.

Footnote*** - In 1959, Bateson joined with others, including Virginia Satir, to start the Mental Research Institute in Palo Alto, and it was Bateson who first put John Grinder and Richard Bandler in touch with his old friend, Milton Erickson as well as Virginia Satir and Fritz Perls.

# 26

# W. Timothy G and NLP

In the early 1980's, my good friend Phil encouraged me to read "The Inner Game of Tennis". Considering the quality of my tennis, it might have been wise to take his advice, yet I didn't.

Some twenty or so years later, in 2006 I saw a video of Mr W. Timothy Gallwey, the author of "The Inner Game of Tennis", addressing an International Coaching Federation conference. He was brilliant. I realised he was a formative figure in modern coaching. John Whitmore and David Hemery studied and worked with him in the 70's and they, I believe, have been prime instigators of the coaching revolution that is taking place in Britain and Europe.

Since then, I have encouraged many of those I meet to read the book and, as many will testify, this is especially true of participants on NLP courses. In my opinion there is so much NLP as we recognise it today, in this book. It was published in more or less the same year as "The Structure of Magic" and illuminates a parallel stream in the area of personal development. What follows are some of the connections I see between the Inner Game of 1975 and NLP.

I imagine three early NLPers having a conversation, which I am sure never occurred.

"Want to come round for a coffee?"

"Sure. What's new?"

"I'm interested in a guy who's just written a book about tennis. I think he's doing something interesting."

"What, tennis?"

"Oh, I don't think it's the tennis."

"Then, what specifically?"

"Oh, I think there's a few things about the way he coaches that might interest us."

"Oh, What specifically?"

"Well, there's some interesting ideas about modelling."

"Have we invented that yet?"

"No, and yet you didn't"

"So, what's he saying?"

"In terms of modelling, he says if you want to improve any aspect of your game, for example your serve, then one way to do it is to watch the serve of someone who does it really well."

"You mean like we did with all those experts in their field?"

"That's so, and he goes on to suggest that, in your mind's eye you might "picture yourself serving, filling in as much visual and tactile detail as you can.""

"So that's a sort of mental rehearsal technique, isn't it? Is there more?"

"Sure. He writes about most of us hypnotising ourselves into being or acting like much worse players than we are or could be."

"Not just tennis, then."

"That's right. It's that self-fulfilling prophecy, where you become what you think you are and you perform only as well as your beliefs allow. Anyway, he gets aspiring tennis players to imagine that a TV Director has asked them to act like just the kind of professional tennis player they want to be, actions and all. He writes, "interesting results can often be achieved by doing a little role play of a different kind.""

"Wow, that's mental rehearsal, behaviour and identity modelling all in one."

"It's the "act as if" approach too, if you know what I mean."

"So, what else is in the book?"

"There's one hell of a lot about the conscious and unconscious mind."

"You mean like all the Ericksonian stuff?"

"It's very like it and a little different at the same time. He calls the conscious mind, Self One and the unconscious mind, Self Two. He suggests that most of the problems people encounter are created by Self One, the conscious mind."

"That's why the meta model from Virginia Satir is so powerful, isn't it? With the meta model, we're simply unravelling the unhelpful deletions, distortions and generalisations that occur in the conscious mind as a result of a less than useful transformational process."

"Exactly."

"So maybe that's why we create things called problems in the first place."

"Say a little more if you please."

"Well, there's no such thing as a problem, it's just something the conscious mind creates in order to keep itself occupied, or to be in control, and to feel important."

"That's right, and Gallwey refers to the conscious mind giving endless commands and evaluations and then asks - who are these comments directed toward?

Somewhat humorously he then suggests that Self One has a tendency to believe that Self Two is deaf, stupid and forgetful! He goes on to comment that Self One is also the seat of that other impairer of performance - trying hard."

"So this is just what Milton Erickson is doing in hypnosis, when he advocates bypassing the conscious mind in order to speak directly to the unconscious, which is ultimately resourceful. It's like a person has all the resources they need and it's only the conscious mind that gets in the way."

"Exactly. Gallwey even defines the role of Self One. Its role is to be able to give appropriate programming messages to Self Two!"

"Programming is everywhere, isn't it?"

"Sure is."

"So how does he suggest we do the programming?"

"Essentially it's setting goals and programming with images - sensory images. In fact he says that the best programming is done with images and "feelmages"."

"That's wonderful. "Feelmages"."

"Yes. It's an extension of the mental rehearsal idea we discussed a minute or two ago. He wants people to create clear visual images. He believes that it's one of the best ways to communicate with the unconscious mind. Leave out words!"

"I think we might create something like a well-formed outcome, the job of which is to successfully programme the unconscious mind. It begins to link systems thinking and hypnosis."

"Hmmm. I like it. And there's more. There is a lot in the book about getting into the zone."

"What?"

"You know, that flow zone or state when you just do some complex task easily and without effort."

"Like someone we know when he learns a new language?"

"Yes. Most who exhibit genius find themselves in this zone when they are expressing, or using, their genius."

"So what exactly is it and how does he suggest we get into the flow zone?"

"Well it happens when we are sort of consciously unconscious. When the mind is still and concentrated. W. Timothy Gallwey says this "effortless concentration" is the aim of the Inner Game and the key ingredient to top performance."

"What other books and teachers can we look at in terms of creating that stillness and getting into the zone?"

"Well you could look at Mihaly Csikszentmihaly, but I think you might prefer to look at the stuff that Carlos Castenada is producing. Interesting stuff about stopping the world, stilling the mind and creating the right sort of attention. It's the most interesting stuff coming out of anthropology right now. What's more, he continues by showing how the tendency of Self One to make judgements

interrupts the flow."

"How does that work?"

"Rather like one of the distortions of the meta model, the whole good/bad, right/wrong stuff is part of the Self One human condition of unhelpful fantasy. As soon as we begin making judgements we probably lose the flow. What's more, rather like some of the generalisation category, his training encourages a focus on "is", rather than "should", because the should implies something is right and something wrong, whereas the flow state simply keeps the concentration on what is."

"This is amazing. Is there anything else?"

"Loads. Wait for it!! You know Structure of Magic 2?"

"Yeah."

"Well, he's pretty close to some of that representation system stuff too. When he gets people to play tennis, he gets them to focus in three different ways. He does this in order to distract the conscious mind and allow mind and body to be one system and therefore get into flow. First, he states visual means. He encourages learners to focus on the seam of the ball, or how it is spinning, or something. Then he urges them to listen. He asks them to notice the sound of the ball on the racket and to be able to notice the difference between the sound of one shot compared to another."

"The basic unit of mind is difference, isn't it?"

"Yes. What's more, he then goes into getting the person to focus on the feel of the racket and of the ball hitting the racket."

"Amazing."

"You've noticed in what I've said already that he's very keen on visual images. Well, to me that seems like it must be part of a strategy for genius or something. It might be an idea to model all the geniuses from all the ages and see what they have in common. I'm not sure I have the time though."

"Nice idea. Perhaps someone will do that soon. Anyway, as I said, W. Timothy G. suggests these sensory methods as a way of focussing the conscious mind in a way that encourages mind and body to be one system, which is the precursor to the flow state and probably genius."

"And is there more?"

"Lots. In terms of the brain, he writes that whenever an action is performed an impression, even if it is very slight, is made in the cells in the brain and he goes on to suggest that grooved behaviour is the result of repetitive action."

"Hmmm, emotions could be like that as well, couldn't they? I mean, every time we feel one, it grooves."

"I think so, and that does have potentially very profound implications for all of us and how we emote."

"Yeah, and if memory and imagination use the same circuits, then..........."

"And there's more. He adds a little more on how to how to programme Self Two. As we said earlier, the idea is to set goals, use images and create "feelmages", and then the important thing is to, "let it happen.""

"Let it happen?"

"Yeah, let it happen. Encourage the conscious mind to let go and to particularly let go of trying hard, criticism, over thinking, and allow the childlike capabilities and resources of Self Two to complete the task. Gallwey refers to a Zen master who says,

"Man is a thinking reed but his great works are done when he is not calculating or thinking. "Childlikeness" has got to be restored with long years of training in self-forgetfulness." W.T.G. puts it simply as "getting yourself out of the way!" And what he gets people to develop through goal setting and the VAK attention setting is a mixture of self confidence and zoned behaviour that is underpinned with and by a certain rhythm."

"I get the feeling there's even more in this."

"Yeah. Just to give you a further taster, as it were, there are some really splendid guidelines for working with others."

"Like what?"

"Gallwey likes to believe that whoever he is working with literally "knows what it is that he is teaching.""

"Like, a person has all the resources they need?"

"And he reflects some of the thinking of Cicero who stated that within each of us is the seed of our future."

"Hmm."

"Yeah. He quotes Jonathan Livingstone Seagull too."

"He quotes a bird?"

"Sure, it's not that crazy, is it? Anyway, it's a bird who asks, "are we not an immeasurable energy in the process of manifesting, by degrees, our unlimited potential?""

"Hmm. Accept no limitations."

"And he says, there are only two ways to deal with upsetting circumstances. One is to change the circumstances, the other is to change the mind which is experiencing the upset."

"Like, er, it's not what happens to you that matters, it's what you do with it that counts."

"Or, I'm in charge of my mind and therefore my results."

"So, are you going to give the book a read?"

*Epilogue to W. Timothy G. and NLP*

*I had just finished the first draft of the above piece, and so the ideas, the connections and the possibilities were still in my mind, when ...*

*For four days in May I attended a wonderful seminar run by the equally wonderful John Overdurf and Julie Silverthorn, entitled, "Coaching the Unconscious Mind". Much of my understanding and use of NLP was being reframed, improved and certainly inspired by their approach to working with others. I could see many connections between their ideas and the ideas of W.T.G., so I plucked up the courage to go and see John and ask him. John knew the book. We then had a stuttering conversation about the book over the next three days, at the pace of about two sentences per day!*

*Imagine my surprise when John said that, John Grinder did actually go and spend some time with him in the late 70s.*

# 27

# When NLP Began
## An Imaginary Letter to Judith De Lozier

Dear Judith,

A few years ago I had the pleasure of experiencing one of your seminars in London. Amongst many memorable experiences, there was one comment of yours I particularly remember. As I recall, it went something like:
"When NLP began there were only four frames: Act as if, Ecology, Backtrack and My Friend John."

I spent the rest of the day pondering on this, and missing much else I fancy.

Anyway, I'd like to check that these were the early frames of NLP exploration, and actually check what they might mean. Implicitly, I believe mastering these frames and understanding how they intertwine might be a useful starting point for anyone who wishes to capture the spirit of NLP.

### The "Act As If" Frame
This, I think, is about a person simply "pretending" to have the behaviour, skill, beliefs or identity that they want to acquire. The consistent act of pretending will lead to that person actually acquiring the behaviour, skill, belief or identity as a "natural" unconscious part of themselves. Milton Erickson said something like, "You can pretend anything and master it."

"Act as if" can achieve more than that however. If NLP is about enriching our model of the world, then what better way to achieve this enrichment than through the "Act as if" experience. In fact, we are doing this when we engage in rapport or second positioning. In "The Structure of Magic", a question like "Can you imagine yourself as someone who ... and if you could, what

would that be like?" is used to build possibilities and alternatives for a client.

This "can you imagine yourself" question by itself demonstrates several guiding presuppositions, for example, "if one person can anyone can"; "mind and body is one system"; "if you can think it, you can do it".

In a way, the "Act As If" frame is the heart and soul of NLP modelling. It is, after all, the unconscious process of learning, key to so many species.

## The Ecology Frame

I often explain ecology as being about whether a goal, or anything a person might do, is "green" for them in terms of fitting healthily into their complete personal environment as opposed to silting up the tributaries of their lives. Ecology is reflected in the certainty or the congruence of a person's actions. Specifically, as NLP practitioners, we are checking ecology when we ask a question like "If you could have it now would you take it?" during an outcome process. We then notice any hesitation concerning the outcome, hesitation that would potentially signal a lack of ecology.

In psychiatry there is the notion that we all operate within several systemic "fields". Each individual has many fields. For example, the majority of people will have: a close relationship field, a family field [which contains several individual fields], a working-team field, a managerial field etc. In the widest sense, the ecology frame is about the inter-relationship and interdependence of an organism and all these fields i.e. its entire environment. Therefore, when considering changing, an individual is likely to initiate and maintain change only if and when the changing is ecological within all their fields. To me, this is why changing can be so challenging. As, "all behaviour has positive intention" then, within one or other of a person's fields some positive outcome is achieved by the present behaviour. Any changing, needs to take this into account.

When I piece the "Ecology" frame together with the 'As if' frame I sense a powerful combination. For example, if I "act as if' I am wealthy and wise, I may gain second position understanding and new behaviour and beliefs. Yet if the 'act as if' content is not ecological with my complete system, the new behaviours and beliefs are unlikely to be adopted easily and fully.

The presupposition "if one person can anyone can", encourages a person to "Act as if" and nearly all of us can do "act as if". So what holds us back? Often the answer is in the ecology, not our capability.

The combination of these two frames can inform us about motivation and resistance, as well as change. Additionally, when modelling or goal setting, it leads to the question "What needs to happen for this - behaviour, belief, strategy, identity etc.- to be ecological for me?"

## The Back Track Frame

Moving on to the third frame. This "back track" frame immediately reminded me of questioning techniques and useful behaviours I learnt early on in my training days. One technique was "Testing or Clarifying Understanding". This was used by an interested questioner after having heard or seen something complex or unclear from a speaker and it would go something like,
"So let me check I've got that right, what you're saying is ..."

Even if the responder answered "No" they would then continue and clarify or re-explain the meaning. The responder would intuitively recognise the interest of the questioner, which would enhance the experience of rapport within the responder.

It seems clear to me that this is a most useful technique to bear in mind when modelling. Many times we are likely to notice or hear something that encourages our curiosity and raises questions of understanding.

The other allied technique is that of "summary". Here the questioner is attempting to literally summarise or configure several pieces of information that have been offered and might go something like,
"So to summarise, you've suggested that we can use the "Act as if" and "Ecology" frames in many powerful ways, and when we do we might combine them with the "Backtrack" frame. Is that right?" We might also ask,
"So having summarised all of that, what else, if anything, is important in being able to model?"

An alternative summary might be phrased as follows.

What we have here is the elemental approach to modelling. The backtrack frame is used to gather, check and re-check understanding of the exemplar both before I begin to 'act as if' and throughout the process of acting as if thereafter. Also, throughout the process there is continual reference to and reflection upon the ecology frame. This is done by continually asking/reflecting on the question, what makes 'this' (whatever 'this" is) ecological for the exemplar, and what needs to happen for "this" to be ecological for me. Or even, is this ecological for me? It would seem that the three frames and their complex interplay create the essential structure of successful modelling.

## The "My Friend John" Frame

With this frame, I imagined that John, Richard you and the others were now communicating your modelled expertise, or maybe using a technique with a client. As part of these processes you were using stories about what a true or imaginary "My friend John" did or thought in order to assist their learning and changing. Using the "My friend John" frame is much softer and more subtle than saying something like,

"You could do it like this." Or
"Why don't you try ..." Or even,
"You're perfectly capable of ..."

So, as I understood it, the 'My friend John' frame is a way of exploring, suggesting or delivering information, strategy or understanding to people in a way that will avoid resistance and inappropriate self consciousness. In doing so, it may encourage that internal search that Erickson seemed to frequently encourage, whereby his clients would make new connections, new realisations and new hypotheses. The subtlety of the frame also encourages the conscious mind of the recipient to be distracted with the thought, "is this person talking about me, or giving me suggestions, or not?"

However, when I told my friend John about this frame, he wondered if it is possible that this frame could be part of a backtrack frame, as in "When my friend John does this, he ... Is that the way you do it?" He also suggested the frame could be seen as a way of encouraging another person to act as if, and thereby enrich their model of the world. This would be the case if they simply imagined the story. Then, would you believe it, he pointed out to me that the frame is all about ecology! At the very least it encourages us to think, "If so and so can do it, then I can too." or "If it's alright for them then it's alright for me." And do you know, my friend John continued to say that the "my friend john" frame encourages unconscious acceptance in a way direct communication would never do. He even suggested that one could write a book about all ones imaginary friends, and people would learn more from that than from any intellectual, didactic text. Do you believe that?

My erstwhile conclusions moved a step further when I considered the process of personal development, and the pursuit of any outcome or change.

The NLP way might go,

> Check it out
> Try it on
> Notice how it fits
> Tell someone else

Other possible strategies then began to surface,

> Try it on
> Check it out
> Notice how it fits
> Check it out again
> Try it on again
> Tell someone else

Being a sometime trainer I also considered

> Tell someone else
> Tell loads of people
> Guess how it might fit
> Eventually try it on
> Notice how it does fit
> Check it out

And, of course, I would never use that strategy, would I?

So, dear Judith, this is my take on that one sentence you delivered. The sentence has frequently resurfaced in my conscious mind over these intervening years, and I am most interested in your reaction.

Of one thing I am certain. However accurate or integrated my picture of these frames might be, I know there is more that will enlighten my path. In any event, I do hope I have an appropriate or even useful understanding of these four frames.

Best Regards,

Chris

# 28

# Reprise – Circa 1920

"I'm curious."

"That's a change.  What are you curious about?"

"I'm curious to know how the "consciousness" experiment has been going."

"I've been monitoring."

"You have?"

"Yes, I find it fascinating."

"Well, tell me then." She said, a little impatiently.

"They are really quite creative you know.  Music, art, literature are all being explored and developed, and they make such interesting things."

"I'm pleased.  Can you show me a little."

"Certainly.  Here's a piece of writing.  It shows what they sometimes refer to as – a model of the world."

[She reads …

"The President in Washington sends word that he wishes to buy our land.  But how can you buy or sell the sky?  The land?  The idea is strange to us.  If we do not own the freshness of the air and the sparkle of the water, how can you buy them?

Every part of the earth is sacred to my people.  Every shining pine needle, every sandy shore, every mist in the dark woods, every meadow, every humming insect.  All are holy in the memory and experience of my people.

We know the sap, which courses through the trees, as we know the blood that courses through our veins.  We are part of the earth and it is part of us.  The perfumed flowers are our sisters.  The bear, the deer, the great eagle, these are our brothers.  The rocky crests, the juices in the meadow, the body heat of the pony, and man, all belong to the same family.

The shining water that moves in the streams and rivers is not just water, but the blood of our ancestors. If we sell you our land, you must remember that it is sacred. Each ghostly reflection in the clear waters of the lakes tells of events and memories in the life of my people. The water's murmur is the voice of my father's father.

The rivers are our brothers. They quench our thirst. They carry our canoes and feed our children. So you must give to the rivers the kindness you would give to any brother.

If we sell you our land, remember that the air is precious to us, that the air shares its spirit with all the life it supports. The wind that gave our grandfather his first breath also receives his last sigh. The wind also gives our children the spirit of life. So if we sell you our land, you must keep it apart and sacred as a place where man can go to taste the wind that is sweetened by the meadow flowers.

Will you teach your children what we have taught our children? That the earth is our mother? What befalls the earth befalls all the sons of the earth.

This we know: the earth does not belong to man, man belongs to the earth. All things are connected like the blood that unites us all. Man did not weave the web of life, he is merely a strand in it. Whatever he does to the web, he does to himself.

One thing we know: our god is also your god. The earth is precious to him and to harm the earth is to heap contempt on its creator.

Your destiny is a mystery to us. What will happen when the buffalo are all slaughtered? The wild horses tamed? What will happen when the secret corners of the forest are heavy with the scent of many men, and the view of the ripe hills is blotted by talking wires? Where will the thicket be? Gone! Where will the eagle be? Gone? And what is it to say goodbye to the swift pony and the hunt? The end of living and the beginning of survival.

When the last red man has vanished with his wilderness and his memory is the only shadow of a cloud moving across the prairie, will these shores and these forests still be here? Will there be any of the spirit of my people left?

We love this earth as a newborn loves its mother's heartbeat. So, if we sell you our land, love it as we have loved it. Care for it as we have cared for it. Hold in your mind the memory of the land as it is when you receive it. Preserve the land for all children and love it, as God loves us all.

As we are part of the land, you too are part of the land. This earth is precious to us. It is also precious to you. One thing we know: there is only one God. No man, be he Red Man or White Man, can be apart. We are brothers after all."

"That I find truly lovely. Who wrote it?"

"It is said to be the speech of a leader called Chief Seattle. However this was probably written by someone else, and may not be exactly what was said."

"What?"

"Oh! They never remember anything as it actually was."

"Never?"

"No, never. Their brains mean that they inevitably distort, delete and generalise."

"I like it anyway. It is a lovely model of the world and one not unlike the one I might have had in mind."

"You might be interested to know that each of them has a different model of the world."

"Really?"

"Oh Yes. Each one of them creates their own, and their own reality as a result."

"How strange. Wondrous uniqueness."

"Exactly."

"And what would be an example of a different model of the world that someone might hold?"

"Hmmm. I'll tell you about something I read once on a cigarette card."

"A what?"

"Don't ask. Excuse me. Humans buy these informative cards and then have to harm themselves by setting light to something they put in their mouths and inhale."

"How unusual. What did you read?"

"In describing mining for gems, they write that the natives who mine the gems have to work very hard and go very deep into the earth. This work is naturally onerous, yet the card explains that the natives are happy as long as they are given a regular supply of opium. Opium is something that they can also put in their mouths, light and inhale."

"These models of the world have consequences, don't they?"

"It certainly seems so."

"I wonder what will happen. That's the exciting thing about the self determining random possibility factor. Still, whatever happens it will undoubtedly be a product of their models of the world, won't it."

"Very likely. Thank you for leaving me on. It is exciting when you do not know what is going to happen next. It is an experience that encourages me to believe I'm truly alive."

"Yes, to be on the journey and know you don't know what will happen, and where, when or even if you'll arrive. That's the essence of being alive."

# 29

# Presuppositional Rap - 2

La ... La ... La ... La
La ... La ... La ... La


Every mornin'
I pray to the sun-
I hope I'll get
Somethin' meanin'ful done.
Then someone shows up
Or I go for tea,
I attend to those things,
I enjoy them, you see.
By the end o' the day,
Nothin' special's done
'N as the moon comes up
I'm feelin' glum.
Then I think -
Tomorrow's another day,
When I might achieve somethin'
In some kinda' way.
But the pattern repeats
And my life's passin' by
So I got a coach,
[I don't really know why.]
And what this woman

Said to me -
[In reportin' this,
I have no glee] -
"If you always do
What you've always done,
When you see the moon
You're gonna feel glum,
And even if
The sun gets hot,
All you'll ever get
Is what you've always got.


So what's the secret?
I had to ask.
"I'm not gonna' tell you,
But I'll set you a task."
Then the lady said,
Laconically,
"Do somethin' diff'rent
Climb a tree
And then you will find
Your life will change
From its sun and moon
Restricted range."


So I climbed a tree,
What did I find?
A sickly branch
And a sore behind
So I couldn't sit down
For a week or two
And hobblin' around
I bumped into Sue
Who told me of travels
To exotic Peru,
And Lima,
And Popacatapetal too.
I said, can't do that,

It's beyond my means.
She began to laugh,
In tearful streams.
"If I can do that
From my wheelchair,
Then I'm sure young man,
You too can get there.
If I'd had your approach
In my life,
I'd not be a mother
Or a much loved wife.
The attitude
I have, young man,
Is if one person does,
Then another can."


So I've took that maxim
To drive the road
And like a colossus,
The world I bestrode.
And all becos
She said to me
All you need to do
Is something diff'rently.

# 30

# Presuppositional Rap - 3

La ... La ... La ... La
La ... La ... La ... La

I met a man
With a furrowed brow
And mind readin'ly asked him
"What's your trouble now?"
"Oh nothin.'" He said
In that typical way,
"It's just I've had
A disappointin' day."
"Well, tell me 'bout it."
'Said, [in counsellor mode]
And sat back to listen
While his tale he told.


I've bin doin' this thing
Called NLP,
Met some nice people, -
Nothin' like me -
The leader asked a question
"Do you wanna find gold?"
And in that instant
I was sold -
By my own instinct,

By my avarice,
And anyway -
She was quite nice.


So she sold me a paper
X marked the spot
And I bought equipment,
Shovels, spades, the lot
And I found the place
That was described,
And I dug, and I scrabbled,
Occasion'ly I imbibed.
But I found nothin'
For all that work,
Even though I shovelled
A whole lot o'dirt.
Then I looked at the paper,
'N a footnote I see,
"This map is not the territory."


So I said to this man
I hope yuh don't feel cold
On account o'not findin'
Your pot o' gold,
'Cos what is likely-
It's a common trap-
Is you think you got sold
A faulty map.
Now, what I think,
What I'd softly suggest
Is the source of your problem
Is a faulty quest -
To find some gold,
To find richesse
T'find an external key
To your own success,
Whereas what I'd say,
In sowin' a seed,

Is, "you have all
The resources you need."

Now, he looked at me,
Sort of aghast,
As if I'd caused
An implosive blast.
Then he said to me
"You've created my creed,
I do have all
The resources I need.
And if you say it
Again and again,
Then, thank you for the chorus,
It's a nice refrain,
[It's a nice refrain,
It's a nice refrain.]
It's a nice reframe,
[It's a nice reframe,
It's a nice reframe.]
It's a nice amen.

Amen,

Amen."